The Catholic Quiz Book

For my brother Mark
of Seddon, Marlborough, New Zealand

and

Paddy Burke
of Bermondsey.
Quizmaster General

The Catholic Quiz Book

Leo Madigan

First published in 1995

Gracewing
Fowler Wright Books
2 Southern Avenue, Leominster
Herefordshire HR6 0QF

Gracewing books are distributed

In New Zealand by
Catholic Supplies Ltd
80 Adelaide Road
Wellington
New Zealand

In Australia by
Charles Paine Pty Ltd
8 Ferris Street
North Parramatta
NSW 2151 Australia

In USA by
Morehouse Publishing
PO Box 1321
Harrisburg
PA 17105 USA

In Canada by
Meakin and Associates
Unit 17, 81 Aurega Drive
Nepean, Ontario
KZE 7Y5, Canada

Cover illustrations by John Ryan.

ISBN 0 85244 2645

Typeset by Action Typesetting Limited, Gloucester
Printed in Great Britain by The Cromwell Press, Wiltshire

Introduction

This little offering is neither a catechism nor an examination paper. I do not imagine that the College of Cardinals jointly could sprint through all one thousand questions without tripping up here and there and stubbing the odd toe along the way.

While compiling it I was often confronted with the unanswerable question, 'What is the purpose of a quiz book?' Is it intended to confound, dismay, amaze or instruct? Should it flummox those with less retentive minds, flatter well-oiled memories, or simply entertain? Perhaps it is because there is a medley of all these motives that the question is unanswerable, at least that is the verdict I arrived at while amassing the information on my kitchen table.

The question and answer format on a particular theme do not occupy the same territory as a radio, pub or board-game type quiz. Be the subject matter Agriculture, Military Hardware or the Literature of Mali one is necessarily addressing The Prepared – reinforcing basics, endorsing principles and introducing aspects which, if not exactly novel, are nevertheless approached by way of unfamiliar streets.

My choice of questions (both Catholic and catholic) is, necessarily, eccentric. I do not apologise for this because I see no alternative; anybody's would be. My aim has been to introduce not simply what intelligent Catholics *should* know, but what they might like to know – even if the information be immediately forgotten. That does not mean the more questions one answers correctly the better the Catholic one must be. To assume so would be tantamount to assessing one's fitness for controlling World Government by the size of one's stamp collection.

If some participants managed to answer 50% of the questions correctly from their store of knowledge (or by guesswork!) I feel they could congratulate themselves for excellence. If they scored more I reckon they may be admirable oddities.

I have not gone out of my way to pose difficult, obscure questions or to practise an eclecticism so refined as to resemble the remoter black holes of algebra. In most cases, when a fact is of interest though it cannot be expected to be common knowledge, I have endeavoured to incorporate clues in the question to enable a reader to make a responsible stab at the answer. As an instance, here is a fact:

St. John of Bridlington, canonised by Pope Boniface IX in 1401, was the last Englishman to be canonised until St. Thomas More and St. John Fisher in 1935. Now, to me anyway, this is an interesting fact and worth a question. The problem is, how to pose it! Thomas More and John Fisher are the subject of several questions already and so I would prefer they were not the answer. The years of Boniface IX's papacy are too esoteric; Pius XI (the incumbent in 1935) is a possibility, but too easy; the dates would require a multiple choice question and this would deflect from the inherent interest of the fact. I am really only left with St. John of Bridlington himself. In my ignorance, I knew nothing of him but, trusting that readers are more enlightened, I researched him in various works of reference and formed the following question:

Which St. John, a Yorkshireman, canonised in 1401, only twenty-two years after his death, was the last English Saint to be canonised before St. Thomas More and St. John Fisher in 1935?

If, like me, you had never heard of St. John of Bridlington there would be no way of guessing the answer, but if you had, then in the 'John' and the 'Yorkshireman' and the date you have some clues. One way or the other the fact that 534 years, over a quarter of the two millenniums of Christianity, elapsed with no Englishman or woman being raised to the altars is of interest. Cynics could interpret it as Roman pique at the Reformation.

Similarly, I have mostly avoided questions like, 'Who wrote *The Imitation of Christ*?' This would be too easy for the readership I envisioned. Instead I have opted for a quote, and often for a date and a nationality, in the hope that the style would suggest the authorship. So too with acronyms and heresies *et al.* but, for the sake of mischief, or simply to let a Greek or Latin scholar shine, I've thrown in esoteric questions without clues. Whether you answer them correctly or no is largely immaterial. My ambition is that interest will be aroused and lead to further reading so that these pages may find a place, albeit among the back shelves marked 'ephemera', of those personal and precious libraries 'haunted by the Holy Ghost'.

Leo Madigan
Fuzeta, Portugal.

Q 1

1 What is the name of the Vatican chapel decorated with frescoes by Fra Angelico depicting the lives of St. Stephen and St. Lawrence?

2 What word is given to the formal ascription of praise to God at the end of a rite or prayer?

3 Who got bogged down in the Slough of Despond?

4 Which religious congregation do the letters C.S.C. identify?

5 Which Hollywood lady, who co-starred with Elvis Presley in *Loving You* and *King Creole*, is now a professed nun in a Benedictine convent in Connecticut?

6 In which sixteenth century classic did the Friar of the Funnels have his prowess vaunted above those of Camillus, Scipio, Pompey, Caesar and Themistocoles?

7 Which volume, a product of medieval Irish monasticism and still extant, is so superbly executed that for long it was thought to have been the work of angels?

8 Of which English Monarch-to-be did a reigning king say that he believed his brother had his mistresses given to him by his confessor for penance?

9 What did the jackdaw 'prig' from the Cardinal of Rheims?

10 Which Joycean character is indicated in the following?:
-- ----- put his face forward to catch the words. English. Throw them the bone. I remember slightly. How long since your last mass? Gloria and immaculate virgin. Joseph her spouse. Peter and Paul. More interesting if you knew what it was all about. Wonderful organisation certainly, goes like clockwork. Confession. Everyone wants to. Then I will tell you all. Penance. Punish me, please. Great weapon in their hands. More than doctor and solicitor. Woman dying to. And I schschschschschsch. And did you chachachachachacha?'

Q2

1   Easter Sunday is a movable feast; by what lunar calculation is its celebration decided?

2   Who was the youngest man to be elected Pope? (eleventh century).

3   Which Italian Passionist preacher received John Henry Newman into the Church?

4   How many Beatitudes are there in St Matthew's Gospel?

5   What is the name of the Jesuit university in Tokyo?

6   Which Lutheran pastor, a colleague of Martin Luther King, became a Catholic priest in 1991? (He is the author of *Doing Well and Doing Good – The Challenge to the Christian Capitalist*.)

7   Which contemporary Catholic writer has a novel (in English) which holds as its premise that the bones of Christ are discovered in Palestine?

8   Who was the first Pope to have his movements captured on cinema film?

9   What medieval liturgy is still in use in a chapel of Toledo Cathedral?

10 Who wrote, in a letter?: 'As to the price of the house, I am not dissatisfied, and you must not be either. I never mind giving a third more than the house is worth for the sake of having one in a good situation; sometimes I have even given as much as half again, for the situation of a convent is so important that it would be a mistake to hesitate about that. In any place I would gladly give far more than this house cost for the sake of water and a view.'

Q3

1 What is the missing word from this sentiment of St. Robert Bellarmine: 'An ounce of peace is worth a pound of - - - - - - - .'?

2 What did St. Pius X in his 1907 encyclical *Pascendi Dominici* refer to as the 'resumé of all heresies'?

3 What, in the Older (Tridentine) Rite, are the four minor orders on the way to the priesthood?

4 What, in the Old Rite, are the four major orders?

5 In an opera Mozart wrote during the same year that he composed his *Requiem Mass*, he celebrated the Masonic alternative to the Mass of the Church. What was the opera?

6 Whose father was disinherited by his father, when he found a Bible in his son's chambers in Oxford, and claimed that: 'he kept not to the Catholique Religion'?

7 Which Spanish mystic (1890–1923) who joined the Society·of the Sacred Heart of Jesus in the Convent of Les Feuillants, Poitiers, was the subject of a book which first appeared in Toulouse as *Un Appel à L'Amour* and the completed edition trans-

lated into English as *The Way of Divine Love* and published in 1949?

8 Which saint wrote in a letter: 'I will give you, however, one piece of advice. There are some things you must hide if you are to appear handsome. Let your nose not be seen upon your face, and let your tongue never be heard in conversation. Then you may, possibly be thought both good-looking and eloquent'? (The correspondent, Onasus, was apparently a windbag, who had had some sort of fourth century nose-job.)

9 What common intransitive verb originally meant 'a pilgrim going to Rome'?

10 Which Englishman, on refusing to sign the Act of Succession in the third decade of the sixteenth century said: 'Not that I condemn any other men's conscience; their conscience may save them, and mine must save me'?

Q4

1 When, to the nearest century, did the Eastern and Western Churches last excommunicate each other?

2 In 1981, in an African town called Kebeho, six girls at a Catholic boarding school claimed to have visions of the Virgin Mary. These were repeated for a year, though one girl is said to have continued to experience the apparitions until 1989. Crowds still gather there. In which country is Kebeho?

3 What famous hymn, used at Compline, is attributed to Adhemar of Monteil, Bishop of Le Puy (1096)?

4 When Vatican II was announced, what political event was holding the world's attention?

5 Its cornerstone was laid in 1163, the facade was completed in 1218, the towers in 1235. It is a cathedral and a basilica built on an island. Can you identify it?

6 What was the profession of St. Alphonsus Liguori before he entered the priesthood.

7 In what year was the first Anglican woman priest ordained?

8 Which former Archbishop of New York has his case for beatification before the Vatican Congregation for the Causes of Saints?

9 What is the theological term for speaking in tongues?

10 When, in 1922, a Hollywood film producer was considering making a life of Christ, which British-born actor told him: 'I want to play the role of Jesus. I'm a logical choice. I look the part. I'm a Jew. And I'm a comedian ... and I'm an atheist, so I'll be able to look at the character objectively'?

Q5

1 Which Cardinal, a leading light in Vatican II, called his autobiography *Memories and Hopes*?

2 Which Pope Gregory introduced the Gregorian Calendar in 1582: Gregory XII, Gregory XIII, Gregory XIV, Gregory XV?

3 What is the annual collection from Catholic communities worldwide on the Sunday in February anticipating the feast of the Chair of St. Peter which is sent to the Vatican Exchequer?

4 What four disasters do the four Horsemen of the Apocalypse represent?

5 When does the first Sunday of Advent fall?

6 Which saint, beheaded in Verulamium around 209 A.D., is considered the first British martyr?

7 What prayer, announced by a bell, is repeated three times a day, morning, noon and evening, in honour of the Incarnation?

8 In 1989 how many R.C. bishops in the U.S.A. were black: 2, 6, 13, 28?

9 What is a Bishop's required five-yearly visit to Rome called?

10 What word is missing from this maxim of St. John of the Cross?: '- - - - - - - is naught but the going forth of the soul from itself and its being caught up in God; and this is what happens to the soul that is obedient, namely, that it goes forth from itself and from its own desires, and thus lightened, becomes immersed in God.'

Q6

1 Name the Council, held between 1438 and 1445, to restore unity between the Latin and Greek Churches? They reached an agreement but were unable to enforce it.

2 By what other three names, in English, is the Sea of Galilee known?

3 What ecclesiastical rank did St. John Fisher hold at the time of his execution on Tower Hill in 1535?

4 Which Italian, born in 1826, was apprenticed to a tailor, became a Redemptorist lay-brother, died at the age of twenty-nine and was canonised in 1904?

5 What psalms are known as the 'Gradual' psalms?

6 What feast of Our Lady is celebrated on July 2nd in the Old Rite and on May 31st in the present Universal Calendar?

7 In which Rite of Holy Mass, still used in some churches in Milan, would the reader, before the Epistle, give the invocation: 'Apostolica doctrina repeat nos gratia divina'?

8 What is the Aramaic word used in the King James and Douay versions of St. Matthew 5.22. which, if any man say it to his brother, shall be in danger of the council?

9 What is the third Sunday before Lent (the ninth before Easter) called?

10 Of which Scottish novelist, born in 1899, is the following passage a representative sample?: 'And hell, according to the theologians, was a very unpleasant place indeed. Sorer than the sorest pain that had ever been suffered in the world and going on forever and ever. "Imagine being simultaneously burned alive and having your nails torn out and your entrails wound through a pronged mangle and having your eyes gouged out and your limbs pulled apart by horses and knowing that the pain would never stop, well, no Gaiety girl's worth that, is she?" Monsignor O'Duffy had once told the men's guild in Tobermory. The Bishop, however, had been inclined to take a more tolerant view. "All we really know about hell is that it is a state that exists," he had once told Father Smith when they had been climbing Ben Nevis

together. 'We know that hell exists because God has told us so and God can neither deceive or be deceived. But we are not bound to believe that there is anybody in it. Even to Judas Iscariot God may have granted the grace of final repentance between his falling from the tree and his bowels gushing out. And even if there are poor unfortunate souls in hell we are permitted, I think, to believe that their agonies are spiritual rather than physical. For the essence of hell is the separation from God, and even unbelievers and sinners shall love God in hell and feel their loss of Him. Indeed, a Spanish priest once told me that he thought it not unlikely that the damned would be punished in hell by being forced to practice for all eternity those very vices through whose indulgence on earth they had forfeited heaven. And sometimes, Father, when out of Christian charity and social politeness I have to listen to the conversation of worldlings, I am not sure that he wasn't right. From an unsupernatural standpoint, the chief grumble that I've got against sin is that it's so boring.'"

Q7

1 What, in traditional spiritual teaching, are the three enemies of the soul?

2 What is the difference between a Religious Order and a Religious Congregation?

3 What English word is commonly used by Catholic writers to indicate the renunciation of apostasy, heresy or schism?

4 Why is a Bull (as in Papal Bull) so called?

5 Which of Evelyn Waugh's characters, in an eponymous short story, gave a party fifteen miles from Ballingar where there was: 'a vast, unfinished Catholic cathedral ... conceived in that irresponsible medley of architectural orders that is so dear to the hearts of transmontane pietists'?

6 Which thirteenth century Dominican, whose work on Conciliar and Papal decrees was to become a standard text among canon lawyers for 700 years, is said to have sailed from Majorca to Barcelona by cloak in six hours?

7 What word is missing from this line of St. John of the Cross?: 'When the evening of this life comes, you will be judged on - - - - .'

8 Nicholas Herman of Lorraine was a seventeenth century Carmelite lay-brother who told that he had been a: '"footman to M. Fieubert, the treasurer," and that he was a "great, awkward fellow who broke everything".' How, and for what, is he better known?

9 In honour of which Catholic writer was a blue plaque attached to the premises of 11 Warwick Gardens, Kensington, in 1965?

10 Which fourteenth century Dominican mystic wrote: 'Suppose a man be hiding and he stirs, he shows his whereabouts thereby; and God does the same. No one could ever have found God; He gave Himself away.'?

Q8

1 Maccabee, a word for a particular tool, was the nickname given to Judas, son of Mattathias (1 Mac. 2:4). It is from Hebrew which, incidentally, gave the word to Greek. What is it in English?

2 What is *Ars Morendi?*

3 When is Shrovetide?

4 Which famous French Jesuit, who claimed Pascal as a paternal forebear, and Voltaire as a maternal one, was ordained in England in 1912?

5 St. Augustine was the Bishop of Hippo. In what modern country is the site of Hippo?

6 What words denote the theory and practice of interpreting the figurative meaning of Holy Writ?

7 With which junior devil was Screwtape in correspondence?

8 What is the doctrine which teaches that after consecration by a priest the elements of bread and wine are transformed into the elements of Christ's body and blood under the accidents (outward appearance) of bread and wine?

9 Which of the twelve apostles is said to be buried in Compostella, Galicia, Northern Spain?

10 Who were the heretics in Southern France from the eleventh to the thirteenth centuries who held Manichean doctrines and followed Manichean practices?

Q9

1 What was the Religious name of Edith Stein, the Jewish-born Carmelite nun who died in the gas chambers of Auschwitz in 1942?

2 Where is the residence of the Coptic Pope?

3 In 1933 an eleven year old girl, Mariette Beco, from the Belgian village of Banneaux, claimed to have a series of visions of a lady who was 'all light'. When Mariette asked the lady who she was, what answer did she receive?

4 Medieval pilgrims wore badges on their hats, around their necks or pinned to their clothes to indicate where they were bound. Pilgrims to Jerusalem were called 'Palmers'. Why?

5 What international Catholic event took place in Montreal, Canada, in 1910?

6 What edict, issued by the Emperor Constantine in 313 A.D., made Christianity a lawful religion?

7 Who coined the word 'Theology'?

8 During the reign of which Cardinal was Westminster Cathedral built?

9 According to tradition, what was the name of the good thief?

10 'No man is an island, entire of itself. Every man is a piece of the continent, a part of the main. If a clod be washed away by the sea, Europe is the less, as well as if a promontory were ... Any man's death diminishes me because I am involved with mankind. And therefore ...' Complete this famous sentence from John Donne's *Devotions upon Emergent Occasions.*

Q10

1 In what Roman Church is there a marble statue by Michaelangelo of Moses seated?

2 What island off the South Wales coast currently houses a Cistercian (Trappist) monastery?

3 What congregation of priests follows the Rule of St. Philip Neri?

4 What order of monks, other than Carthusians, lives the hermetic life in monasteries?

5 Which fifteenth century English poet, a convert to Rome, wrote:
'How life and death in
Thee Agree!
Thou hadst a virgin womb,
And tomb.
And Joseph did betroth
Them both'?

6 Holland lost her Catholic Hierarchy under the Calvinist governments of the sixteenth century. In which decade of the nineteenth century was it restored?

7 What is the philosophical doctrine according to which all matter possesses life?

8 Which Pope was condemned as a heretic by the sixth General Council in 680 A.D.: Boniface IV, Honorius I, Boniface V, Honorius II?

9 Which twentieth century English King, upon ascending the throne and addressing parliament for the first time, refused to abide by the tradition of declaring as 'superstitious and idolatrous' the invocation of the Virgin Mary and the Sacrifice of the Mass?

10 Which great seventeenth/eighteenth century French preacher and Archbishop, later condemned for Quietism, wrote: 'If God bores you, tell Him that He bores you, that you prefer the vilest amusements to his presence, that you only feel at ease when you are far from Him.'?

Q11

1 Which twentieth century Pope said, and on what occasion: 'The substance of the ancient deposit of faith is one thing, and the way in which it is presented is another.'?

2 What is the title of the short anonymous Russian work discovered on Mt. Athos in 1884, translated in full into English by R.M. French in 1941 and reprinted many times by S.P.C.K.?

3 In what year was divorce made legal in Italy: 1919, 1938, 1965, 1970?

4 Which Bishop was entirely subservient to Henry VIII, spying for him in Rome, Ambassador for him in Spain and Germany, supporting the divorce and taking the Oath of Supremacy, yet resisted the changes made by Somerset and Cranmer? He was imprisoned, but when Mary Tudor acceded he took possession of his Diocese, London, and was staunch in restoring every emblem of Catholic life.

5 *Atone* is probably the only theological term with an English origin. What is the adverbial phrase it derives from?

6 In the nineth chapter of St. Luke's Gospel, why would the people of a Samaritan village not entertain the disciples who had been sent ahead to make preparations for Jesus' visit?

7 Which contemporary Prelate wrote: 'Where there is neither consensus on the part of the Universal Church, nor clear testimony in the sources, no binding decision is possible. If such a decision were formally made, it would lack the necessary conditions, and the question of the decision's legitimacy would have to be examined.': Ratzinger, John Paul II, Suenens, Hume?

8 Name the Sorrowful Mysteries of the Rosary.

9 Who wrote this of the infant Christ?:
   'He was so small you could not see
   His large intent of courtesy.'

10 Which would-be Pope had a cat called Flavio?

Q12

1   What names are commonly given to the Wednesday, Thursday, Friday and Saturday before Easter Day?

2   Which Irish born, nineteenth century woman, known as the 'Mother of Orphans', has a public statue erected in her honour in New Orleans, Louisiana?

3   What is a *Lipsanotheca*?

4   What is the teaching in Moral Theology, but not favoured by it, which says, in effect, that one must favour a law against liberty and, when laws conflict, one must favour a law opposed to natural inclinations: Rigorism, Laxism, Reflexism, Tutiorism?

5   During what year did the first apparition occur at Lourdes?

6   What is the sixth Sunday in Lent called?

7   What was the medieval Church institution which forbad private war on Friday, Saturday and Sunday of every week under pain of excommunication?

8   Which country, in 1967, proclaimed itself the first atheistic state in the world?

9   What name is given to the view that there are three Gods, as opposed to the Three Persons in One God of the Trinity?

10   Which nineteenth century born priest, a convert to Catholicism, whose father was Archbishop of Canterbury and whose mother was described by Gladstone as 'the cleverest woman in Europe' wrote, in his introduction to Lady Lovat's *Life of St. Teresa*: 'Religion is not one department of life, like art or biology; it cannot be segregated from the rest of our experience without ceasing to be true to itself; it is, on the contrary, either the sum of the whole of life, affecting or being affected by every single incident of life, or it is not true religion at all.'?

Q13

1 Who played Jesus in Pasolini's 1964 film *The Gospel According to St. Matthew*:
   Fabio Gregori, Marcello Mastioianni, Carlo Martorini, Enrique Irazoqui?

2 What is the name given to the European movement of Catholic Intellectuals?

3 In what year was St. Teresa of Avila made a Doctor of the Church:
   1699, 1796, 1889, 1969?

4 In what year did the English translation of the post Vatican II Mass appear?

5 What animal did Jesus call Herod?

6 Which Franciscan contemporary of St. Francis was sent to Karkoum in Central Asia on a mission to the Mogul Khan, travelling 3,000 miles in 106 days:
   Friar Ascelinus, John of Plano Caprini, Andrew of Longjumeau?

7 Which contemporary Italian actor/playwright wrote the satirical play *The Pope and the Witch*?

8 In which part of the former Yugoslavia is the pilgrim town of Medjugorje?

9 What is a zuccheto?

10 Mary of Agreda, Catherine of Siena, Catherine Emmerich, Faustina Kowalska. Through which of these visionaries did Christ speak the following words: 'The watch-dog of conscience, so enfeebled, begins now to bark so loudly that he leads the soul, as it were, to despair; but all should lay hold with hope on the blood, in spite of the sins which they have committed, because my mercy which ye receive in the blood is without any comparison greater than all the sins which are committed in the world.'?

Q14

1 What name does Genesis give to the land, east of Eden, where Cain went after he murdered Abel?

2 How many Popes ruled from Avignon in the fourteenth century:
2, 5, 9, 11?

3 Who wrote the poem *The Dream of Gerontius*, later put to music by Elgar?

4 Who was St. Benedict's sister?

5 Under which Roman emperor's persecution was St. Agnes put to death:
Diocletian, Nero, Heliogabalus, Caracalla?

6 What is the plate that holds the Eucharist during Mass called?

7 What provocative and humorous name did Daniel O'Connell call Sir Robert Peel when the latter attacked the Irish Catholic leaders?

8 What was the dogma that precipitated the German speaking Old Catholics break with Rome in 1870?

9 Who was the Harvard Law Professor who led the Holy See Delegation to the United Nations Fourth World Conference on Women in Beijing in September 1995?

10 Name the Bavarian town where a Passion Play is staged every ten years?

Q15

1   When was the *New Catechism of the Universal Church* first published: 1989, 1990, 1991, 1992?

2   Which Pope's corpse, in 897 AD, was withdrawn from its sarcophagus, seated on a throne and charged with (later discredited) irregularities. Found guilty of having been unworthy of the Pontificate, all his measures annulled, the Papal vestments torn from the body, the three fingers he had used in consecrations severed, the body cast into the strangers' grave, and after several days thrown into the Tiber?

3   With which contemporary, one time Dominican, do we associate the Institute of Culture and Creation Spirituality in Oakland, California?

4   Which Englishman was one of the original founders of the Cistercian Order in 1098?

5   What radical decision did the Church of England make on 11th November 1992?

6   What contemporary Catholic presence marks the remembrance of those hanged at Tyburn gallows?

7   Who painted the record of the Council of Trent that hangs in the Louvre: Titian, Peruzzi, Michaelangelo, van Eyck?

8   What is a triduum?

9   What word did the desert hermits give to the lethargy and spiritual dryness they used to suffer from?

10 Which Catholic Cornishman, born in 1548, was a member of Elizabeth I's court, purportedly refused the queen's advances, had his estates confiscated, was imprisoned for twenty-eight years, released and banished by James I, assigned a pension by the King of Spain, had eighteen children by his wife, died in Lisbon in 1608 and whose body, disinterred seventeen years later, was found to be incorrupt?

Q16

1 On his accession what title did Henry VIII bestow on the Blessed Margaret Pole, mother of Reginald, later Cardinal, Pole?

2 Which three of the sacraments can only be administered once validly?

3 The American evangelist Billy Graham first preached in a Catholic Church in Poznan, Poland. What was the year: 1968, 1973, 1978, 1983?

4 When the 2934 enfranchised of Vatican II voted against the reversal of clerical celibacy what was the ratio for and against: 1468:1466, 1956:978, 2614:320, 2930:4?

5 When was Pope Paul VI's encyclical *Humanae Vitae*, reiterating the Church's ban on birth control issued?

6 What title did John Bunyan give to his autobiography?

7 Who said of Christ: 'You see, there is nothing you can do; look, the whole world is running after him.'?

8 Which thirteenth century French cathedral has a gallery of monarchs in its great doorway – forty-two statues of former Kings of France?

9 Who baptised St. Augustine?

10 Who wrote in *De Moribus Divinis*: 'It is another of the ways, or perfections, of God that he judges no man according to his past or future wickedness or holiness; but according to the present state of his soul. Thus He did not condemn Paul on account of his past malice, nor did he save Judas on account of his former justice.'?

Q 17

1 When Pius IX declared Papal infallibility in 1870, was the infallibility retrospective?

2 Which sect, mentioned by Augustine, sprang up in North Africa in the second and third centuries, called their churches 'Paradise', condemned marriage as not observed by Adam, and practiced nudism in common worship?

3 Which fictional pagan actor, favoured by Diocletian, in searching for a key to play a Christian martyr, in a play within a play, himself became a Christian and a martyr?

4 Why was the 1525 reform of the Franciscan Order called Capuchin?

5 What is the difference between a peal of bells and carillon?

6 Where can we hear a prayer which starts: 'Oh God, by whom the dignity of human nature was wonderfully established.'?

7 What are the missing words from this sentence of the sixteenth century Swiss writer Paracelsus: 'God will do nothing without - - - . If God works a miracle he does it through - - - .'?

8 What is the ornament of pure gold, blessed by the Pope on Laetare Sunday, and conferred from time to time on eminent Catholics as a token of Papal esteem?

9 Which American female playwright was married to the founder of *Time*, *Fortune* and *Life* magazines, became a Catholic in 1946 and was appointed U.S. Ambassador to Italy in 1953?

10 What Greek-based name is given to a liturgical book containing the lives of the saints, arranged by months throughout the liturgical year?

Q18

1 Which Bohemian professor (1370–1415) protested relentlessly against the wealth and unspiritual conduct of prelates, papal politics and simony, was condemned as a heretic at the Council of Constance and burned at the stake: Konrad Kyeser, John Huss, Eric of Pomerania, Ivan Sisman?

2 In medieval English monastries a boy was hired to turn the spits, carry fuel and catch fish from the ponds. What was he called: A turnbroach, a chuff, a mooncalf, a rummer?

3 In what American play of 1934, set in a Jesuit house, does a miracle, which is not a miracle, save the vocations of two priests, and a miracle, which is a miracle, do the same thing for a third?

4 What was the nickname given to Sister Pasqualina, the housekeeper of Pius XII, who wielded so much power in the Vatican between 1939 and 1958?

5 What is a 'fane'?

6 Nellie Organ (24th August 1903 – 2nd February 1908 i.e. four and a half years) of Waterford, Ireland, suffered greatly and with a religious fervour that astonished those who came in contact with her. She was permitted early communion and, after her death, when her body was being transferred (1909) it was found to be incorrupt, the fingers quite flexible and the garments intact. What was she better known as?

7 Excommunication *vitandus* (i.e. one to be shunned or boycotted) is only incurred automatically by one act. What is the act?

8 What is a Cathedraticam?

9 After which St. Bernard are the Augustinian hospices of the Great and Little St. Bernard Passes (and the dogs) named: Bernard of Vienne, Bernard of Clairvaux, Bernard of Feltre, Bernard of Menthon?

10 What two words are missing from this quotation from Origen: 'Christ does not baptise with water; this He leaves to the disciples. He reserves to Himself the power to baptise with the Holy ------ and with ---- .'?

Q19

1   The city of Hierapolis is mentioned in Colossians 4:13. Today it is a Turkish tourist attraction because of its calcium terraces. What do the Turks call it?

2   What was the medieval sisterhood, under simple vows but not enclosed, known as?

3   What word, coined in the nineteenth century from 'Exegesis', means interpreting a biblical passage to suit one's own ideas?

4   What word is missing from this scholastic axiom: '- - - - - does not disregard or destroy nature; it presupposes and perfects it.' – grace, peace, order, unity?

5   What canonical hour is traditionally associated with the massacre of the French at Palermo on 30th March 1282?

6   Name the influential monastic order, chiefly but not exclusively in Spain and Portugal, founded in the fourteenth century.

7   What is the branch of theology which deals with the art of preaching?

8   What is the shawl worn by the priest when holding the monstrance for benediction or in a procession called?

9   In what Biblical city were there: '12,000 people who couldn't tell their right hand from their left, to say nothing of the animals.'?

10   Which Hindu mystic (initials S.S.S.) embraced Christianity at the beginning of this century but, the mutual exclusiveness of the various Christian bodies being incomprehensible to him, maintained an undenominational position saying: 'The children of God are very dear but very queer – very nice but very narrow.'?

Q20

1 What is the prolongation of a festival for eight days called?

2 Who took St. Peter's place as head of the Church when he died circa 48 AD?

3 What is a person called who has, or professes to have, an intuitive apprehension of spiritual truths?

4 What are the *Apophthegmata Patrum*?

5 What are the nine charismatic gifts?

6 Which fourth/fifth century Doctor of the Church wrote that he valued marriage because it caused virgins to be born?

7 What is the (unlikely and non-physical) word missing from the following quotation from the seventh century East Syriac Isaac of Nineveh: '"What is a compassionate heart?" He replied, "It is a heart on fire for the whole of creation, for humanity, for the birds, for the animals, for - - - - - - and for all that exists. At the recollection and at the sight of them such a person's eyes overflows with tears."'?

8 How many Popes have been assassinated?

9 Which President of the United States of America said: 'Sir, my concern is not whether God is on our side; my great concern is to be on God's side.'?

10 Which famous Englishman stole, in the 1590s, the prized library of Mascarenhas, Bishop of Faro, later Grand Inquisitor of Portugal?

Q 21

1 When Andrew asked Jesus where he lived, what did Jesus answer?

2 Which seventeenth century canonised visionary is Christ said to have called: 'the beloved disciple of the Sacred Heart and the heiress to all its treasures'?

3 The only contemporary Carthusian monastery in the British Isles is St. Hugh's Charterhouse in Cowfold, Sussex. It is named after the twelfth century St. Hugh, Bishop of Lincoln. Why?

4 What word describes any person, not a professed monk, friar or nun, who has been offered to God, or who has been dedicated to His service, in Religion?

5 When Rome established the American (U.S.) Hierarchy in 1808, what city was designated as the Archiepiscopal See?

6 What, traditionally, is said to have been the name of the Roman soldier who pierced the side of the crucified Christ with a lance?

7 What was the name of the Curé d'Ars?

8 Where was Jezebel eaten by dogs?

9 Who founded the Samaritans in 1953?

10 Which seventeenth century English poet called prayer:
'Exalted manna, gladness of the best,
Heaven in ordinarie, man well drest,
The milkie way, the bird of Paradise,
Church bells beyond the stars heard, the soul's bloud,
The land of spices; something understood.'?

Q22

1   What is the Sunday after Easter called?

2   In Ronald Knox's story, who: 'will lecture in the Albert Hall at 3pm on The New Sin, recently discovered by him and now for the first time brought to the notice of the public. All seats free.'? (Clue: think Belial.)

3   Who wrote the hymn *Anima Christi*?

4   St. Francis of Assisi was born Giovanni di Pietro di Bernardone. How did he acquire the name Francis?

5   Which Fathers of the Eastern Church were known as 'The Three Cappadocians' or 'The Cappadocian Fathers'?

6   What is the word used to denote the enclosure of the Cardinals at a Papal election, as ordered by Gregory X in 1274?

7   What is the missing word, more used in medical surgery, in this sentence by Gabriel Marcel (1889–1973) in *Being and Having*: 'But this detachment (poverty, chastity etc.) must not be a mere - - - - - - - - - -; everything which is shaken off must be found again at a higher level.'?

8   What was the subject of Benedict XV's 1936 encyclical *Vigilanti Cura*, addressed to the Bishops of the United States: Economic hardship, The Motion Picture industry, Gangster warfare, Nocturnal worship?

9   Who was the most recent non-Italian Pope (*Pontifice Barbaro*) before John-Paul II?

10 Which famous, or notorious, French Cardinal (1585–1642) wrote, with reference to preserving an even keel between the political policies of the Gallicans and the Ultramontanes: 'One must neither believe the people of the palace who ordinarily measure the power of the King by the shape of his crown which, being round, has no end, nor those who, in the excesses of an indiscreet zeal, proclaim themselves openly as partisans of Rome.'?

Q23

1 What prayer, originating with the Franciscans in the thirteenth century, was introduced as an admonition to Catholics to pray for the victory of the crusades?

2 What fourth century spiritual writer is responsible for *Piers Ploughman?*

3 From the pen of which British writer on Vatican affairs, and former Jesuit, did the following come: 'Hans Küng says he loves the Church not as a mother but as a family. I wonder what he means by this distinction. I suppose he is rejecting the idea of "Mother Church" ... Yet whoever heard of a family that consisted only of co-equal brothers and sisters? Is it not possible that in rejecting Mother Church and all fatherhood including that of the Holy Father we are losing an essential dimension? The Church exists not only horizontally in space, but vertically in time as tradition and handing on. There is a danger in throwing out not just the baby with the bath water but the grandmother as well.'?

4 Two Catholics, father and son, were Lord Mayors of London (1892–3 and 1909–10). What was their family name:
   Wall, Knill, Tell, Mills?

5 St. Ambrose said: 'The knee is made flexible, by which offence against the Lord is mitigated, wrath appeased, grace called forth.' What name do we give to the physical action he is talking about?

6 What incident from Exodus is the subject of paintings by Tintoretto in S. Giorgio Maggiore, Venice; Poussin, in The Louvre, Paris; Bacchiacca, in the National Gallery, Washington; and Dick Bouts, in St. Pierre, Louvain:
   The Bloodying of the Lintels
   Moses receiving the commandments,
   The Worshipping of the Golden Calf,
   The Gathering of the Manna?

7 Who first uttered the words *Nunc Dimittis?*

8 What single Latin word occasioned the split between the Eastern and Western Churches?

9 Name the one European

language to have main-
tained the ecclesiastical
nomenclature for the days
of the week – Dominica,
Feria secunda etc., Italian,
Portuguese, Romanian,
Spanish.

10 Who is the patron saint of
speleologists (cave explor-
ers)?

Q 24

1 Daniel O'Connell died in Genoa in 1847. His body was returned to Ireland but, by his own request, where was his heart sent?

2 Who was the last Anti-Pope?

3 Where is the world head-quarters of Charles de Foucauld's Little Brothers of Jesus?

4 What is the parish church for the residents of Vatican City?

5 What are the opening words, and therefore the name by which it is known, of Pius XI's encyclical to mark the fortieth anniver-sary of *Rerum Novarum*?

6 Apart from the use of the vernacular, in what radical way has the recitation of the psalter in the breviary been changed since Vatican II?

7 Which of John of Gaunt's grandsons has been beati-fied?

8 What two animals are missing from this quotation from the Swiss theologian, Karl Barth: 'He who does not believe in universal salvation is an - - ; but he who dares teach it is an - - - .'?

9 How many Catholic churches are there in Nepal: 0, 1, 15, 23?

10 Which Gluck opera, thought by many to be his master-piece, is set during the First Crusade under Godfrey de Bouillon?

Q 25

1   What is the girdle used to confine the loose flowing alb as a Mass vestment called?

2   In what year did the Oxford Movement in the Church of England begin: 1829, 1833, 1845, 1846?

3   Why did Clement V set up the Papacy in Avignon in the early fourteenth century?

4   Which wealthy Catholic lady, a character of Evelyn Waugh's, said: 'It is possible for the rich to sin by coveting the privileges of the poor.'?

5   How long did Daniel stay in the lions' pit:
    Three days and three nights, two days, one week, overnight?

6   Why is the fourth century St. Elmo (or Erasmus) the patron of sailors?

7   If you ascribe human characteristics to things that are not human, such as saying that God sits in the heavens or that angels have golden hair, what 'ism' are you using?

8   Which Catholic writer, who died in 1991, had a book recording his dreams published posthumously?

9   What two subjects were forbidden by the British Board of Film Censors in 1913 and have never been formally revoked?

10 What is the Church's marriage tribunal called?

Q26

1. The *Sanctuario del Miraculo* in Lanciano, Italy, lays claim, with a considerable body of historical evidence, to the first recorded Eucharistic miracle. It holds that in the eighth century a monk, harbouring doubts about the Real Presence, found himself at Mass with a Host changed into recognisable flesh and wine into recognisable blood. These are still reserved in the sanctuary and have been often subjected to scientific scrutiny which has attested to their authenticity. The question here is, what is Jesus' blood group:
   A, B, O, AB?

2. Who is the patron saint of cancer sufferers?

3. '*At the cross her station keeping*': What is the Latin title of the hymn of which this is the first line?

4. Which Abbot of Bec in Normandy did William Rufus appoint to the See of Canterbury?

5. In 1573 when the artist Paolo Veronese was summoned before a tribunal for painting buffoons, drunkards and Germans (i.e. Protestants) in his *Last Supper*, what course did he take to appease his accusers?

6. In which 1944 film did Gregory Peck and Vincent Price appear together as priests?

7. Which heresy asserted that Christ's human body was a phantasm, and that his sufferings and death were appearance, arguing that if He suffered He could not be God, and if he was God he could not suffer?

8. Which eighteenth century Italian Saint prayed incessantly for the re-conversion of England and had visions and revelations about its final re-admittance to the fold?

9. St. Raymond (1200–1240) was called Nonnatus. Why?

10. Which Belgian pilgrimage town was given a monstrance by Henry VIII?

Q27

1   When St. Bernadette asked the Lady at Lourdes who she was, what answer did she receive?

2   What was the slogan of the fifth–sixth century Theopascite controversy:
    God was crucified,
    One of the Trinity was crucified,
    One of the Gods was crucified,
    All the Trinity was crucified?

3   What was the name given to Bismark's policy of anti-clericalism following Vatican I's proclamation of Papal Infallibility?

4   George Joseph Camel (or Kemel) (1661–1706), from Moravia, became a Jesuit lay-brother and was sent to the Philippines where, in addition to his missionary activities, he turned his hand to botany and sent the results of his investigations back to Europe. Why, in this field, is he remembered today?

5   What early Christian labyrinthine construction would, if laid in a straight line, extend the length of Italy?

6   What, after the fall of Communism did Hans Küng call 'the last authoritarian absolutist institution in Europe'?

7   In 1990 how many bishops were there worldwide: 1,900, 3,440, 3,907, 4,210?

8   Which doughty lady (1880–1958) chained a copy of her disapproving book *Roman Catholic Methods of Birth Control* to the font of Westminster Cathedral?

9   What is the correct pronunciation of the word 'Schism': sizm, skism, schtism, szizm?

10 Which Eastern Father wrote in *De Incarnatione Dei*: 'You know what happens when a portrait that has been painted on a panel becomes obliterated through external stains. The artist does not throw away the panel but the subject of the portrait has to come and sit for it again, and then the likeness is re-drawn on the same material.'?

Q28

1 What is the name (from a saint's feast of that day) given to the bloody massacre of Huguenots on August 24th 1572 in which between 16,000 and 30,000 (sources differ) lost their lives?

2 What is a treaty between the Papacy and a temporal power concerning ecclesiastical affairs called?

3 What are the synoptic gospels?

4 What was an earlier word for a pulpit?

5 On what day is the blessing and distribution of candles traditional?

6 Which saint is the patroness of music?

7 Which English writer and broadcaster who died in 1990 at the age of eighty-seven wrote a book called *Conversion; A Spiritual Journey* after he became a Catholic?

8 What did the early Christians call their Eucharistic meal?

9 Name the Augustinian monastic ruin, in the Black Mountains of Wales, that has a pub built into it?

10 Which contemporary comedian claimed in one of his many books to be 'the worst Catholic since Ghengis Khan'?

Q29

1 Which five organs are anointed during the sacrament of the Anointing of the Sick?

2 What is the published announcement, verbal or written, of a proposed marriage in an R.C. church?

3 What are the periods of fasting to mark the four seasons called? (i.e. the Wednesday, Friday and Saturday following December 13th, Ash Wednesday, Whitsun and 14th September.)

4 'Is it not, then, a happy augury that today's meeting takes place in that land where Christ founded His Church and shed His blood for her.' What was the ecclesiastical status of the man to whom these words were addressed by Pope Paul VI in Jerusalem on January 5th 1964?

5 Which fictional character, the creation of a French philosopher, was put in handcuffs and subsequently hanged at an *auto-de-fé* in Lisbon for having said: 'Free will can subsist together with absolute necessity, for it was necessary that we should be free.'?

6 In which book of the Old Testament did Jael, the wife of Heber, drive a tent peg, or nail, through the brain of Sisera as he lay asleep, pinning him to the ground?

7 What is the collection of spiritual writings by the Fathers of the Eastern Church from the fourth to the fourteenth centuries, existing in Greek, Slavonic and Russian versions, called?

8 Which Dalmatian Catholic Primate and Archbishop turned against Rome (he owed large sums of money), embraced Anglicanism, was welcomed at the Court of James I in 1617, was made Dean of Windsor and Master of the Savoy Chapel, made a lot of money, and enemies, returned to Rome vilifying the Church of England, was knuckled by the Inquisition and holed up in the castle of Sant 'Angelo in Rome where he died a natural death:

Marc' Antonio de Dominio,
Maximilian of Trauttmansdorf,
Podiebrad,
Ernest de Hesse -Rheinfels?

9   In what Hitchcock film did
    the actor Edmund Gwenn
    fall from the top of
    Westminster Cathedral?

10 What is the black cloth
    spread over a coffin or
    catafalque called?

Q30

1 Who founded the Ursulines?

2 How many R.C. Bishops function in Scotland:
    9, 12, 19, 27?

3 What name was given to the early heretical sect, later absorbed by Manichaeism, which rejected the Old Testament in the belief that Christ was not the son of the God of the Jews, but the son of a greater God:
    Ebionites, Cerinthians, Sabellianites, Marcionites?

4 To what religious order did the somewhat dissolute painter Fra Filippo Lippi belong before being released from his vows to marry?

5 What is the doctrine, declared heretical in the sixth century, which holds that all men will be saved?

6 Which Hungarian pianist and composer (born in 1811), after a varied life which included many mistresses, took minor orders in his early fifties and functioned as an Abbé for twenty-one years before his death in 1886?

7 Who had published, in 1926, a novel called *Concerning the Eccentricities of Cardinal Pirelli*?

8 When was the ecclesiastical law regulating Papal elections enacted:
    903, 1059, 1685, 1831?

9 Bishop Fridelin Zàhradnik has the distinction among contemporary Roman Catholic Bishops of:
    Being canonised in his own life time,
    Sporting an ear-ring,
    Holding a degree from the University of Antarctica,
    Having ten grandchildren?

10 The following quotation is from *The Prayer of Love and Silence* (1962): 'God would not be infinite Goodness and Wisdom if, seeking and even demanding our love, He had not at the same time made it possible for us to enter into this intimacy with Himself.' The book acknowledges no individual authorship because to do so is against the policy of the Religious Order to which the author belongs. What is the Order?

Q31

1   Thomas Merton's auto-biography was published in England under the title *Elected Silence*. What was it called when first published in the USA?

2   What virtue does the delightfully cynical Ambrose Bierce define as 'A brief preface to ten volumes of exaction'?

3   Which Byzantine Emperor started the iconoclastic persecution in 726 AD:
    Anastasius II, Theodosius III, Leo III, Constantine V?

4   '"From the Church Militant and Triumphant we sever thee."
    "Nay! From the Church Triumphant thou canst not."'
    This was the reply of a fifteenth century Dominican preacher to excommunication. He claimed that he was being excommunicated on political rather than on religious grounds. He was subsequently burned at the stake. Who was he?

5   What is the death of the Blessed Virgin called in devotional parlance?

6   What Papal title alludes to the doctrine that he is the representative of Christ as head of the Church on earth?

7   Where did the Biblical Job come from?

8   Which early Doctor of the Church wrote: 'We are told that her first husband was a man of such heinous vices that even a prostitute or common slave could not have put up with them ... The Lord ordained that a wife must not be put away except for fornication ... a command that is given to men applies logically to women. It cannot be that an adulterous wife should be put away and an unfaithful husband retained.'?

9   Of which Belgian Benedictine Abbey was Dom Marmion, author of *Christ the Life of the Soul* etc, Abbot?

10 What version of the Old Testament, translated into Greek in the centuries before Christ by seventy or so Jewish scholars, is considered the most important of all available versions?

Q 32

1 Between what years did the Second Vatican Council sit?

2 What Religious Order runs a retreat house in Hazelwood Castle in Tadcaster, North Yorkshire:
   Passionists, Carmelites, Dominicans, Franciscans?

3 Who was the first missionary to preach Christianity in Japan?

4 What body, convoked by Emperor Charles V, issued the 1521 edict condemning Luther?

5 Who was the companion and emanuensis of Jeremiah?

6 What name was given to the French Protestants of the sixteenth century?

7 Who was the last R.C. Bishop of Iceland to be executed by the Reformation forces:
   Bjârna Gereksson, Hallgrim Gíslason, Jón Thorlaksson, Arason Jón of Holar?

8 Against whom did Dr. Achilli, an ex-Dominican and anti-Popery lecturer, bring a libel action in 1852?

9 What does the following sentence define: 'The extra-sacramental remission of the temporal punishment due, in God's justice, to sin that has been forgiven, which remission is granted by the Church in the exercise of the Power of the Keys, through the application of the super-abundant merits of Christ and of the saints, and for some just and reasonable motive'?

10 Which canonised Bishop of Geneva wrote, in *Letters to Persons in the World*: 'The world is only peopled to people heaven'?

Q 33

1. Which fifteenth century Council declared that General Councils of the Church possessed an authority superior to that of the Pope in matters pertaining to the Faith, the ending of schism, and the reform of the Church?

2. In church architecture what, usually, is a semi-cylindrical projection roofed with a half dome?

3. St. Margaret Mary Alacoque's stigmata reflected only one facet of Christ's passion. What was it?

4. Cardinal Rgwamba of Tanzania was the first native African to be created Cardinal. In what year: 1932, 1949, 1952, 1960?

5. **To** what noted musical composition did George Bernard Shaw refer in this extract: 'I have long since recognised the impossibility of obtaining justice for ------'-, ------- in a Christian country.'?

6. St. Patrick's Seminary in County Kildare, about twelve miles from Dublin, is commonly called after the village adjacent to it. What is the name of the village?

7. What were Christ's last words on the cross?

8. For whom did the American press coin the phrase 'Cafeteria Catholics'?

9. Who played the part of the 'whisky priest' in the 1947 film of Graham Greene's *The Power and the Glory*?

10. Which eighteenth century Catholic poet and satirist wrote, in a letter: 'The greatest magnifying glasses in the world are a man's own eyes when they look upon his own person'?

Q34

1 Who wrote the Hymn *Lead Kindly Light*?

2 What order did St. Norbert found in 1120?

3 St. Bridget of Sweden (1303–1373), claimed that Christ revealed to her the number of blows he received during his scourging. How many were there:

   328, 1,101, 3,719, 5,480?

4 Which English representative said to the Roman Synod of Bishops in 1987: 'The people of God travel through history on bread and butter, not caviar, and because of this it is important to look at the local churches as the arena for change, not Rome.'?

5 In early Christian architecture a part of the church was separated from the nave by a low wall or screen and reserved for catechumens and penitents who were not admitted to the congregation. What was this area known as?

6 On what date do we celebrate the feast of the Immaculate Conception?

7 What was the basis of the Biblical measure, the cubit?

8 What is the meaning of the word 'Christ'?

9 Define eschatology?

10 What very well known work ends with the following: 'I shall bring my own work to an end here too. If it's well composed and to the point, that is just what I wanted. If it is trashy and mediocre, that is all I could manage. Just as it is injurious to drink wine by itself, or again water, whereas wine mixed with water is pleasant and produces a delightful sense of well-being, so skill in presenting the incidents is what delights the understanding of those who read the story. On that note I will close.'?

Q35

1 Who was the canonised grandmother of Madame de Sévigné, the seventeenth century writer whose letters stand as models for the epistolary genre?

2 What is the name of the Benedictine Abbey on the Isle of Wight?

3 Which country enjoyed the *Monarchia Sicula*, a right that it had from the early sixteenth century until it was revoked in 1871, by which the secular rulers had final jurisdiction in purely religious matters, independent of the Holy See?

4 What is the status of the Parish Priest of the Falkland Islands' only Catholic church, in Stanley?

5 Which nun wrote, quoting her sister: 'After my death you must not speak about my manuscript until it has been published ... otherwise the devil will set traps for you so that he may spoil God's work.'?

6 Supply the missing words from this sentence of Nicholas of Cusa, a fifteenth century German Cardinal: 'God is a circle whose centre in - - - - - - - and whose circumference is - - - - - - - - - -.'

7 What is the apposite and Biblically based name of the church in Milton Keynes, opened in 1992 in the presence of the Queen, the Cardinal Archbishop of Westminster, the Archbishop of Canterbury and other Church leaders and is shared by a number of Christian disciplines?

8 The monks of which English Benedictine Abbey wear white habits in honour of Our Lady, as opposed to the black habits generally worn by the order?

9 Name the Religious Congregation, formerly an Anglican foundation which embraced Roman Catholicism *en bloc* in 1909, which runs the Catholic Central Library in London?

10 Which English Catholic journalist (1919–1981), of Irish extraction, and for a number of years on the staff of the *Observer* newspaper, wrote the following: 'They do it every morning. They are dressed in a modified and decorated version of the outdoor clothes of the rich in Imperial Rome. Their utensils stand on stones that contain calcified fragments

of those who are believed to
have been killed because
they refused to live a lie.
They do it in colossal cathedrals, on kitchen tables, in
chapels built on the cheap,
at baroque altars in which
an instant of religious drama
has been frozen in stone
and contrived light, in
rooms over public houses
that still smell of beer and
occasionally, still, in upper
rooms with the doors
guarded. A man bends over
a piece of unleavened bread
and over a silver gilt cup
with a little wine and water
in it and he pronounces a
formula more terrible than
the sound of guns. Hoc est
enim, it runs in part, Corpus
meum. And the majority of
Christians believe that God
Himself is immediate and
present, not in the way that
He is everywhere anyway,
but in a way that a man is
there in the same room.'?

Q36

1   What lady, notable in her own right, was Leonard Cheshire's wife and fellow convert?

2   Bearing in mind the dispute over Adam's navel, can you guess, if you are not already familiar with the work, what is noteworthy about the devils represented in the painting *The Story of Job* by the Master of the Legend of St. Barbara (1482?) in the Wallraf-Richart Museum in Cologne?

3   Which Pope refused to sanction Henry VIII's divorce from Catherine of Aragon and marriage to Anne Boleyn?

4   What honour was vouchsafed to Alderman Francis Taylor of Swords, Mayor of Dublin in 1595, and Margaret, the wife of Bartholomew Ball who was Mayor of Dublin in 1553, on September 27th, 1992?

5   Which Edinburgh working girl, who died in 1925, was declared 'Venerable' in 1978?

6   Which contemporary Catholic M.P., notable as champion of many causes, and notably anti-abortion, wrote, in 1992: 'I am not bound hand and foot by the dictates of a Church demanding my obedience. But I *am* aware of the Christian message and of my Church's interpretation of it. A Christian in politics – and a Jew or a Muslim would doubtless say the same – is not a pilgrim without a map.'?

7   In the Eastern Churches, Orthodox and Uniate, what word is used to correspond with our word 'Diocese'?

8   What, in the penny catechism, are the four last things?

9   Which thirteenth–fourteenth century Dominican theologian is known as 'The Father of German Mysticism'?

10 What structure, 31ft × 15ft in a basilica near Ancona, Italy, is purported to have been the house of the Holy Family at Nazareth?

Q 37

1 Which great Swiss Benedictine Abbey, named after an Irish monk a companion of St. Columban, suppressed in 1805, had written above the door of its famous library, in Greek, *Medicine Chest of the Soul*?

2 What are the opening words of the Tridentine Rite of Mass?

3 Are there any Roman Catholic communities among the monastic enclaves of Mt. Athos?

4 In which great Christian poem, part of a trilogy, is the name of Christ not mentioned once?

5 What name do we give to the Eucharist as administered to the dying?

6 In 1634 a group of Belgian Jesuits started a literary work called *Acta Sanctorum* which, despite scores of volumes, has still not been completed. What overall name is given to the writers of this mammoth task?

7 Near which ancient fortress were the Dead Sea Scrolls found in 1947?

8 A contemporary European farmer called Biernacki, born in 1922, whose gift of healing has been demonstrated on many occasions, has published a series of dire prophecies concerning the future of the world. What country does he come from?

9 What is the missing word from this sentence of William Hazlitt: 'Defoe says that there were a hundred thousand country fellows in his time ready to fight to death against - - - - - - , without knowing whether - - - - - - was a man or a horse.'?

10 Which Englishman (1596–1666), considered to be the last of the great Elizabethan dramatists linking the Golden Age with the period of Restoration, took Anglican orders at Cambridge but soon converted to Catholicism? His dirge beginning 'The glories of our mortal state are but shadows, not substantial things' is said to have terrified Cromwell. He and his wife died on the same day while fleeing from the Great Fire of London.

Q 38

1 What is the name of the Syrian Uniate Church, prominent in Lebanon which, having come into contact with the Crusaders in 1182, accepted the supremacy of the Pope and has been in communion with Rome ever since?

2 Who founded *Opus Dei*?

3 Which famous Jesuit saint was the great grandson of the notorious Pope Alexander VI?

4 Who, in 1962, said of what: 'It is like a big ship; I have launched it; others will have to bring it home to port.'?

5 In what country was the Franciscan saint, known as St. Anthony of Padua born? He spent the greater part of his life there.

6 By what name is the former Converts' Aid Society now known?

7 What are the Seven Gifts of the Holy Spirit?

8 To what Religious Congregation of priests did Jean-Bertrand Aristide of Haiti belong?

9 What is the name given to the branch of study which has the saints as its object?

10 The same word is used eight times in the following passage from Max Picard. What is it?: 'If ---- did not make its dwelling in man, it would be much more ---- than it is. ---- cannot be as ---- as it wills to because it is tied to man. Because it is in man, a watch is kept on ----. In man, the image of God, ---- is constricted; it is there under custody as in a prison. The destructive power of ---- would be unlimited if it were on earth alone, unsheltered by God's image. The earth is saved from destruction because, in God's image, a watch is kept upon ----.'

Q39

1 What well known heresy in the early church taught that the Son of God was a creature of similar, but not the same substance as, the Father?

2 At what age does a Cardinal cease to be eligible as an elector in the conclave to elect the Pope?

3 In what year was the Polish Solidarity priest Jerzy Popieluszko murdered in Warsaw:
  1978, 1980, 1982, 1984?

4 What ecumenical body does the acronym CCBI represent?

5 What office did St. Ambrose, St. Charles Borromeo, Pius XI and Paul VI hold in common during their lifetimes?

6 Bishop Fulton Sheen contributed an introduction to the 1949 Everyman edition of a translation by Edward B. Pusey D.D. of a classic, in which he stated: 'No other Latin book, with the exception of Virgil, has been translated into so many languages and read over such a long period of time.' What was the work?

7 What is the title of the rightly famous sermon (Lord Macaulay was said to have known it by heart) John Henry Newman delivered to the first Provincial Synod of the restored Hierarchy of England and Wales at Oscott in 1850?

8 Which French cleric was the first Vicar-Apostolic to be appointed to New Zealand, in 1836?

9 What English noun, from the supine of the Latin verb *offero* is, unlike 'offer' almost exclusively restricted to matters religious?

10 In which extra-liturgical service is the hymn *Tantum ergo* sung?

Q40

1 Name the notorious Nazi slaughtercamp where Carmelite nuns set up a convent before being forced to move?

2 Where do the Popes traditionally live from July to September?

3 Which British writer did the Vatican send to Mexico in the 1930s to report on the state of religion there, a journey which resulted in the book, *The Lawless Roads*?

4 Where is the home of the Apostolic Nuncio to Great Britain?

5 A decree of Urban VIII on 21st September 1624 reads, in part: 'Let every (Religious) Order have private - - - - - - -, at least one in every province.' What is the missing word?

6 Which British observer, and later Catholic convert, witnessed the bombing of Nagasaki from an American B-29 on 9th August 1945?

7 The episcopal palace of what city was used to shoot the opening scenes of the Miles Forman film *Amadeus*?

8 What shrine in Norfolk, England, has been a major place of pilgrimage since the time of St. Edward the Confessor?

9 What word, taken from the Italian, is used to indicate that a Cardinal, or indeed any baptised Christian, would make a credible Pope?

10 Where, in Poland, is the Marian shrine of Jasna Gora?

Q41

1 What is a chartulary?
2 Define Tenebrae.
3 What is simony?
4 What is defined as 'an enclosed space for religious retirement'?
5 In a country without an established ecclesiastical hierarchy what is the Bishop of a District called?
6 What is the Pope's 'cabinet' of Cardinals called?
7 What is a basilica?
8 What is the screen at the back of an altar called?
9 Of what race was Og the King of Bashan, who had an iron bedstead nine cubits by four, the last survivor?
10 Which former Communist wrote in his autobiographical *Now I See*: 'The emotional revivalist often produces valuable effects, but all revivalist movements are subject to the law of diminishing returns. It is impossible for men to live forever on the heights. A religion which equates the emotional state with salvation is a broken reed when the temperature drops.'?

Q42

1 How is an Apostolic Delegate formally addressed?

2 What was the last doctrine to be made an Article of Faith?

3 Name the Bishop of Galway who, in 1992, resigned because it was disclosed that he had fathered a son and used diocesan funds for the boy's upkeep.

4 What are the twelve Fruits of the Holy Spirit, listed in the Douay/Rheims Bible, as mentioned by St. Paul in Galatians 5:22–23? (N.B. The Gifts are the source, the Fruits are the stream.)

5 Who is the author of the 'Brother Cadfael' series of detective books set in a medieval monastery?

6 Who was the longest reigning Pope?

7 What Archdiocese in northern Portugal has its own liturgical Rite?

8 What sacramental activity did Pius X's 1905 encyclical *Sacra Tridentina Synodus* encourage?

9 Which Monarch was on the British throne when the Gunpowder Plot was to have been executed?

10 Which grandson of Noah, son of Japhet, is said to have populated the Iberian peninsula and has a Portuguese city named after him?

Q43

1   Who was the Archbishop who would not accept Vatican II and held the Church to be heretical?

2   Name the Spanish city with a shrine to Nuestra Señora del Pilar which, tradition claims, originated in apostolic times when St. James set up a statue of Our Lady there?

3   Whose wife was Caroline Sargeant (d.1837)?

4   Which thirteenth century theologian is noted, among other things, for saying: 'I thought it more likely that a cow would fly than a monk would lie'?

5   What did Ambrose Bierce define as: 'A preposterous form of religious error, perversely preferred by three fourths of the human race'?

6   Which of Paul Claudel's religious dramas, performed over four days, ends with a character called Brother Leo saying: 'Deliverance for all souls in prison'?

7   What Bull of Leo XIII on the 15th September 1896 declared the Anglican orders to be invalid 'in form and intent'?

8   Which Florentine Dominican painter refused to make any alterations to his pictures believing that his hand was guided by God, always prayed before taking up his brush, and shed tears of contrition whenever he painted Christ crucified? He was beatified in the 1980s.

9   Which poem of Francis Thompson did Coventry Patmore hail as 'one of the few *great* odes of which the language can boast'?

10 To which sixteenth–seventeenth century figure did the Church formally apologise and retract denunciations of in October 1992?

Q44

1 In which Spanish city is the Royal Scots College seminary?

2 Which two nineteenth century writers, one Scottish and the other American, by their writing established Father Damien of Molokai's true position in the esteem of the public after the Rev. Dr. Hyde questioned his morality?

3 What is the statutory age for the resignation of a Bishop?

4 In Rubens's *Adoration of the Magi* what animal, not usually associated with Nativity scenes, is prominently depicted?

5 What is the Religious name of the woman who founded The Little Sisters of Jesus along the lines of Charles de Foucauld's rule?

6 What was Father Malachy's Miracle?

7 What are the Eastern Rite Churches in communion with Rome called?

8 Canon John Gray (b.1866) a Catholic priest of St. Peter's, Morningside, Edinburgh, is said to have been the original model for which of Oscar Wilde's characters?

9 What is the name of the island, visited by Pope John Paul II on a visit to Senegal in 1992, once used to house slaves waiting for traders to carry them to the Americas?

10 What are the three largest churches in Europe?

Q45

1 What is the aromatic resin *Boswellia sacra* known as in the scriptures?

2 In what year did Godfrey de Bouillon take Jerusalem: 1026, 1099, 1128, 1189?

3 What are the four Cardinal Virtues? (They are also called the Moral Virtues.)

4 St. John Gualbert founded the Vallumbrosian order of cenobitic monks in the eleventh century. What Burne-Jones painting is based on an incident of his pre-monastic life?

5 Name the ecclesiastical tribunal instituted in 1229 to deal with heretics?

6 Did Pope Innocent III welcome or deplore the Magna Carta in 1215?

7 Which celebrated English novelist, in the 1840s, spent two years translating David Friedrich Strauss' *Life of Jesus* for which she was paid £20?

8 Which English saint, in his prescription for a relatively perfect society, wrote: 'Before marriage some grave matron presents the bride naked whether she is a virgin or a widow, to the bridegroom, and after that some grave man presents the bridegroom naked to the bride.'?

9 In which decade of the last century were the Little Brothers of Mary, or Marist Brothers, founded, and by whom?

10 The following is taken from the second century *Protreptikos*, from the Greek 'to persuade', a book dealing with the awakening of the pagan soul:
'Just take a look at the servants of their idols:
Filthy hair, soiled and torn clothes,
They are total strangers to the bathtub,
Their nails are like claws of wild animals.
Many of them are even emasculated.
These facts show that the sacred precincts of the idols
Are nothing more than tombs or prisons.
Some people mourn their Gods instead of honouring them.'
Which of the Alexandrian Fathers wrote it?

Q 46

1 Who wrote the hymn *O Salutaris Hostia*?

2 In which year was Mother Teresa of Calcutta awarded the Nobel Peace Prize?

3 May a person receive the sacrament of the anointing of the Sick when in danger of death from external causes, such as imminent execution of a death sentence?

4 What congregation of priests was founded in Algiers in 1868 by Archbishop, later Cardinal, Charles Lavigerie (1825–1892).

5 What are the three progressions of the Communion of saints?

6 What are the nine titles of the Pope as listed in the *Annuario Pontifico* – the official Vatican directory?

7 What happened to Herod Antipas or 'The Tetrarch' (murderer of St. John the Baptist and involved by Pilate in the Passion drama) four or five years after the death of Jesus?

8 What is breakfast called in a Cistercian monastery?

9 Which nineteenth century English Jesuit described himself as 'fortune's football'?

10 Frater Felix Fabri, a Dominican, went to the Holy Land in 1483 and wrote a book about it. Here is an extract. What animal is he talking about: 'Surely this beast appears to me to be more amazing than any other beast on earth, for a man may hardly depict the form and habit of body of that same beast. Six years old he was at the time and he was of the largeness of a horse ... but altogether ungainly. He has nor hair, nor mane, nor bristles, but looks bald, he keeps his head bowed like a pig, little eyes like a pig.'?

Q47

1　In the Sermon on the Mount what did Christ promise would be the reward of the peacemakers?

2　By what act is a person incorporated into the Body of Christ?

3　What word is missing from this sentence of Robert Hugh Benson in *The Conventionalists*: 'If a mistaken marriage can be purgatory, a mistaken - - - - - - - - is hell.'?

4　What is the origin of the term 'left-footer' to identify a Catholic?

5　What is the word used, chiefly in a Biblical context, for a manifestation of God in the convulsions of nature: earthquake, lightning, thunder, clouds, smoke, wind etc?

6　What organisation did Mrs. Cornelia Connelly, *née* Peacock, of Philadelphia, USA, found in Derby, England, in 1846?

7　Was Jesus buried inside or outside the walls of Jerusalem?

8　What is the Latinization of Holywood, as in the name of the Irish Jesuit Christopher Holywood (1559–1626).

9　In what London Church has it been traditional to bless those suffering from throat infections on St. Blaise's Day, February 3rd?

10　From which English mystical work is the following extract taken: 'And right as this little word FIRE! stirreth rather and pierceth more hastily the ears of his hearers, so doth a little word of one syllable, when it is not only spoken or thought, but secretly meant in the depth of the spirit, the which is the height; for in ghostliness all is one, height and depth, length and breadth. And rather it pierceth the ears of Almighty God than doth any long psalter unmindfully mumbled in the teeth. And therefore it is written that short prayer pierceth heaven.'?

Q 48

1 Which nineteenth century English Prelate wrote the hymn which begins:
   'Full in the panting heart of Rome
   Beneath the Apostle's crowning dome,
   From Pilgrim's lips that kiss the ground,
   Breathes in all tongues one only sound,
   God bless our Pope.'?

2 Which sixth century Bishop of Paris has a suburb and a soup named after him?

3 What is the title of the first – not canonical or apocryphal – authenticated Christian book (first and second century) consisting of five visions, twelve mandates and ten parables? Its opening lines are: 'He who brought me up sold me to a certain Rhoda, who was at Rome. After many years I met her again and began to love her as a sister.'

4 What scattered pieces of Papal, Conciliar and Diocesan legislation were brought together by the *Decretum Gratiani* in 1142, have since been added to and amended, and are today be defined as 'the body of laws and regulations made

by or adopted by ecclesiastical authority, for the government of the Christian organisation and its members'?

5 The Jesuits, in common with most male Religious communities founded since the sixteenth century, are not monks or friars. By what name do we identify them?

6 The famous statue of Christ the Redeemer in Rio de Janeiro, Brazil, stands dramatically on an outcrop of rock called *Morro do Corcovado*. What does *Corcovado* signify in English?

7 What name is given to the belief that there are innumerable spiritual beings concerned with human affairs and capable of helping or harming men's interests?

8 Name the seven hills of Rome.

9 What was the name of Pope John XXIII's famous last encyclical dealing with human rights, the dignity of the individual and international harmony?

10 Who is the Doctor (canonised in 1323) referred to here: 'after the death of the Doctor, Brother Reginald,

having returned to Naples and resumed his lectures, exclaimed, "My brothers, while he was still in life my Master forbade me to disclose the admirable things concerning him whereof I had been witness. One of these things was that he had acquired his science, not by human industry, but by the merit of prayer, for whenever he wished to study, read, write or dictate, he first had recourse to prayer in private, and poured forth his soul in order to discover the Divine secrets, and by the merits of this prayer his doubts were removed and he issued therefrom fully instructed."'?

Q49

1 How many General Councils has the Church convened since, and including, the Nicean Council in 325: 17, 21, 30, 32?

2 What Latin word is used for the narrow-necked bottles, which belly out like a jug, in which medieval pilgrims carried the oil from shrines?

3 Who was Mary Stuart's first mother-in-law?

4 Give the family name of St. Térèse of Lisieux?

5 Whom did Pope John Paul II visit in Rome's *Rebibba* prison on December 27th 1983?

6 Name the Prince Cardinal and Prince Primate of Hungary, born under Habsburg rule, who was arrested for treason in 1948 and tortured for twenty-nine days by the Communist Secret Police, being made to stand naked in a cold, damp cell, beaten with a rubber hose and forced to witness obscene orgies? Released in 1956 he spent fifteen years in the US Embassy in Budapest, he was finally dismissed as Primate after criticising the Pope's attempts to deal with the Hungarian regime and died in Vienna in 1975.

7 Which BBC TV programme satirised Vatican II in 1962 by portraying a group of Cardinals singing *Arriverderci Roma*?

8 Where was the following sentence to be found on 31st October 1517: 'The difference between Hell, Purgatory and Heaven seems to be the same as that between despair, almost despair and confidence.'?

9 What is the name of the ancient Marian shrine in Austria, about ninety miles from Vienna?

10 Which Catholic writer (1874–1936), defined paradox as 'truth standing on its head to attract attention'?

Q50

1. What are Bishops who are independent of a Metropolitan called?

2. Which riverside street in Chelsea, London, has a blue plaque on the exterior wall with the words: 'Hilaire Belloc (1870–1943), poet, essayist and historian lived here 1900–1905.'?

3. How many days did Pope John Paul I spend in office: 30, 33, 39, 41?

4. What was singular in the learning of Giuseppe Meofanti (1774–1849), son of a carpenter of Bologna and priest there until, in his sixties, he was brought to Rome and created Cardinal?

5. What is the name given to the upper room where the Last Supper took place?

6. Which Capuchin saint, who died in Lisbon in 1619, was baptised Julius Caesar?

7. Who was the first US Cardinal?

8. Which saint, author of the Marian classic *True Devotion to the Blessed Virgin* wrote the following: 'To Mary, His faithful spouse, the Holy Ghost has communicated His unspeakable gifts; and he has chosen her to be the dispenser of all He possesses, in such sort that she distributes to whom she wills, as much as she wills, and when she wills, all His gifts and graces. The Holy Ghost gives no heavenly gift to men which he does not pass through her virginal hands. Such has been the will of God, who has willed that we should have everything in Mary; so that she who impoverished, humbled and hid herself, even to the abyss of nothingness by her profound humility all her life long, should now be enriched and exalted by the Most High.'?

9. What is a mixture of the resins of rock-rose (cistus) and nees (balsamodentron) better known as in the Bible?

10. Which Cambridge professor, who also wrote novels under the pseudonym 'Q', wrote, or rather, lectured, on the English of the Bible: 'We will go on to imagine that all the poetry is written as prose; while all the long paragraphs of prose are broken up into short verses, so that they resemble the little passages set out for parsing or analysis in an examina-

tion paper ... Having
effected all this, let us
pepper the result over with
italics and numerals, print it
in double columns, with a
marginal gutter on either
side, each gutter pouring
down an inky flow of references and cross references
... It remains then only to
appoint it to be read in
churches.'?

Q51

1   Which Holywood actor did the narration for the film *Quo Vadis*?

2   What is the compilation of the four gospels into a single narrative called?

3   Which saint's famous prayer begins: 'Make me, O Lord, an instrument of your peace'?

4   If a penitent is solicited for sexual purposes by a confessor, Canon Law requires the penitent to denounce the cleric to the Bishop of the diocese in which the penitent lives. If the penitent, without sufficient cause, does not make the denunciation within a month from the time that he or she has learned of the obligation to do so, what penalty is prescribed?

5   With reference to the foregoing question, if anyone falsely denounces a confessor on the charge of solicitation, what penalty is attached?

6   The first cinemascope film on public release was *The Robe*, from a novel concerned with the fate of Christ's seamless garment. Who wrote the novel?

7   What age was Pope Leo XIII on his death in 1903: 93, 97, 99, 101?

8   Where is the Latin Rite Archdiocese of Naxiensis Tinensis?

9   Which American poet, author of the often anthologised *Trees*, was received into the Church in New York in 1913 and killed in action in France in 1918?

10 Which seventeenth century, Anglo-Welsh, metaphysical poet wrote:

'I saw eternity the other night,
Like a great ring of pure and endless light,
All calm, as it was bright;
And round beneath it,
Time, in hours, days, years,
Driven by the spheres,
Like a vast shadow moved.'?

Q 52

1 Which 1951 English drama is set in a church where the four protagonists dream they are Biblical characters?

2 In Byzantine iconography what is the meaning of the word *hodegetria* which is used of the Madonna pointing to the infant Christ?

3 What is the term used for the lists naming persons being prayed for during the Mass?

4 In what year did the custom of Thanksgiving Day start in the USA:
1591, 1621, 1721, 1821?

5 What Gothic church in Wellington, New Zealand, built in 1921, gained a certain notoriety in 1992 by advertising abroad for funds to restore it?

6 Who started the original (English) Catholic Truth Society in the 1860s?

7 In Canon Law what ages must the man and the woman have reached for a marriage to be valid?

8 According to an article in the *British Medical Journal* in 1958 by Arnold Sorsby, quoting the Book of Enoch and a fragment of the Dead Sea Scrolls, what physical phenomenon was Noah subject to:
A leper, A consumptive, A paraplegic, An albino?

9 What familiar phrase alludes to a solemn form of excommunication used in the medieval Church?

10 From which great Greek preacher, called 'the Golden-mouthed', is the following taken: 'God desired a harlot, and how doth He act? He doth not send to her any of His servants. He doth not send any angels or archangels, cherubim or seraphim. No, He himself draws near to the one He loves, and He does not take her to heaven, for He could not bring a harlot to heaven, and therefore He himself comes down to earth, to the harlot, and is not ashamed. He comes to her secret dwelling place and beholds her in her drunkenness. And how doth He come? Not in the bare essence of His original nature, but in the guise of one whom the harlot is seeking, in order that she might not be afraid when she sees Him, and will not run away, and escape Him. He comes to the harlot as a

man. And how does He
become this? He is
conceived in the womb, He
groweth little by little, as we
do, and has intercourse with
human nature. And He
finds this harlot thick with
sores and oppressed by
devils. How doth he act? He
draws nigh to her. She sees
Him and flees away. He
calleth the wise men, saying,
"Why are ye afraid? I am not
a judge but a physician. I am
come not to judge the
world, but to save the
world." Straightaway He
calleth the wise men, for are
not the wise men the immediate first fruits of His
coming? They come and
worship Him, and then the
harlot herself comes and is
transformed into a maiden.
The Canaanite woman
comes and partakes of His
love. And how doth He act?
He taketh the sinner and
espouseth her to Himself,
and giveth her the signet
ring of the Holy Ghost as a
seal between them.'?

Q53

1 Under what other title was Graham Greene's *The Heart of the Matter* published?

2 Which nineteenth century American novelist wrote: 'Better to sleep with a sober cannibal than a drunken Christian.'?

3 What was, or is, a veil worn by women approaching the Communion Rail called?

4 In May 1969 Rome dropped thirty-one saints of doubtful historicity from the Universal Liturgical Calendar. Who was the best known and the most exhorted?

5 Which Uniate Byzantine rite has traditionally used Arabic in its liturgy?

6 On August 4th 1914 Britain declared war on Germany, standing by the 1839 treaty guaranteeing Belgian neutrality. On the 20th German troops took Brussels. What significant event took place in the Vatican on the same day?

7 When is *Cantate* Sunday?

8 Which famous sculptor (of the 'Three Graces') was sent to Paris in 1815 as the Pope's envoy to negotiate the return of the art treasures Napoleon had carried off from Italy during his campaigns?

9 What was the purpose of the official German rewriting of the Psalms in 1934?

10 What words are missing (the same root in both cases):

'Then arose new architects who, after the manner of barbarous nations, erected buildings in that style that we call - - - - - - .' (Vasari)

'The ancient Greek and Roman architecture answered all the perfections required in a faultless and accomplished building but the - - - - - destroyed these and introduced in their stead a certain fantastical and licentious manner of building; congestions of heavy, dark, melancholy monkish piles, without any proportion, use or beauty.' (Evelyn)?

Q54

1 Which Jacobean dramatist was 'twelve years a Papist'?

2 What is the missing word from this quotation by Whitgift, in Dr. Johnson's Dictionary under the letter 'P': 'A great number of parishes in England consist of rude and ignorant men, drowned in - - - - - - - -.'?

3 Graham Greene's fictional character John Callifer hanged himself and was resurrected. In what manner of building did this event take place?

4 What nationality was St. Dominic?

5 On what day is the feast of St. Andrew, Patron Saint of Scotland, celebrated?

6 On January 8th 1904 the newly elected Pius X criticised the low-cut evening gowns of diplomats wives. Which French heroine, now Saint, had he beatified the day before?

7 Which Italian tenor married Miss Dorothy Benjamen in St. Patrick's Cathedral, New York, in 1918?

8 What degree of consanguinity is forbidden in the Cardinalate?

9 Which former novice of St. Bernard of Clairvaux became Pope:
Lucius II, Eugene III, Anastasius IV, Hadrian IV?

10 Four quotes from a nine-teenth–twentieth century English language novelist. Who was he?:
1) (1899) 'A Church should be like a rock in the middle of the ocean – unmoved. The mad individualism of Nietzsche, the exaggerated altruism of the next man tainted with selfishness and pride come with their noise and froth, pass away and are forgotten. Faith remains; ... Truth is immovable – it is eternal, it is one; and a Church as the repository of the highest truth cannot listen, cannot absorb what is unstable, complex and doomed to die.'
2) (1900) 'It is strange how I always, from the age of fourteen, disliked the Christian religion, its doctrine, ceremonies and festivals ... and the most galling feature is that nobody – not a single Bishop of them – believes in it.
3) (1914) 'The base from

which he (Tolstoy) starts –
Christianity – is distasteful
to me. Great, improving,
softening, compassionate
it may be but it has lent
itself with amazing facility
to cruel distortion and is
the only religion which,
with its impossible stan-
dards, has brought an
infinity of anguish to innumerable souls.'
4) (1923) 'I was born
Roman Catholic, and
though dogma sits lightly
on me I have never
renounced that form of
Christian religion. *The
Book of Rules* (of an
Anglican club he had been
invited to join) is so, I may
say, theological that it
would be like renouncing
the Faith of my Fathers.'

Q 55

1 What is a canopy over an altar called?

2 The following is a quote, used elsewhere in this book, with its sixteen words listed alphabetically. Rearrange them to find the quote:

   a do does God God he If it man. man. miracle, nothing through without will works

3 The first Papal visit to South America was by Paul VI in August 1968. At what city did he first touch down?

4 Which British painter, who died in 1992, produced a series of bizarre 'popes' based loosely on Velàsquez's *Innocent X*?

5 What is an alternative word for reincarnation, or transmigration, of souls?

6 The mother of which great saint of the Anglo-Saxon Church was said to have been forewarned of the sanctity of the child within her when, in church on Candlemas Day, all the lights were inexplicably extinguished. Then the candle held by the mother-to-be burst into flame and all present took their lights from it, foreshadowing that the child 'would be the minister of light' to the English Church?

7 What was the name, a colour, given to the laws regulating personal conduct and the observance of the Sabbath in the State of Connecticut in 1646?

8 Who is considered the 'Apostle of the (Antillian and South American) Indians'?

9 What, in the weekly routine of a Carthusian, is the *Spatiamentum*?

10 Which work of John Dryden finishes with Raphael saying to Adam and Eve:

   'The feebler herd before the stronger run;
   For now the war of nature is begun:
   But, part you hence in peace, and having mourned your sin,
   For outward Eden lost, find Paradise within.'?

Q56

1 Can ordination to the priest-hood be annulled?

2 In which Maurice Maeterlinck play did a nun leave her convent, and a statue of the Virgin come to life to take her place?

3 On 4th October 1965 Paul VI became the first Pontiff to visit the Western Hemisphere. What was the purpose of his journey?

4 What is the principle of economy which says that 'entities are not to be multi-plied beyond necessity' known as, and what connec-tion has it got with the Franciscans?

5 In Lytton Stratchey's *Emminent Victorians* of which convert cleric is it said, 'had he lived in the Middle Ages would certainly have been neither a Francis nor an Aquinas, but he might have been an innocent'?

6 Which oddly named king and kingdom appear in both Ezekiel and in the Apocalypse?

7 Under whose portrait, preserved at Gertruidenberg, are written the words: 'Everywhere I have sought rest and found it nowhere, save in little nooks with little books'? (The original is a charming mixture of Latin and old German: '*In omnibus requiem quaesivi et nusquam inveni nisi in een Hoecken met een Boecken*'.)

8 What painting of the Blessed Virgin on poor sacking, presumably executed by heavenly means on 12th December 1531, has given its name to a famous shrine?

9 What is the study of the feasts of the Christian calendar called?

10 Which part of a ship is named after the fact that religious statues used to be housed there for the devo-tion, and protection, of the sailors?

Q57

1 In 1990 how many ordained R.C. priests were there world wide:

    403,173, 517,862, 712,123, 1,127,298?

2 What writings are referred to in these missing words from Leo XIII's *Providentissimus Deus*: 'The sense of ------ ---------- can nowhere be found incorrupt outside of the Church, and cannot expect to be found in writers who, being without the true faith, can only gnaw at the bark, and never attain its pith.'?

3 Before visiting Calcutta in December 1964, what gift did Pope Paul VI make to the world's poor?

4 When Mussolini escaped the fourth attempt on his life in 1926 who observed: 'This is a new sign that Mussolini has God's full protection'?

5 What is the canonical difference between nuns (*moniales*) and sisters (*sorores*)?

6 While Henry VIII was defying the Pope and marrying Anne Boleyn in London what notable event, purportedly in the name of the Faith, had just taken place in Peru?

7 What is a heresimach?

8 What is the Hebrew meaning of the word *Hosanna*?

9 Which lawyer, in 1679, said to the hangman at Tyburn: 'I am desirous to be with my Jesus. I am ready and you need stay no longer for me.'?

10 What did the following have in common: Bogomiles, Piphles, Jovinians, Turlupins, Petrobrussians, Speronists and Picards?

Q58

1 What is the distinctive outer vestment of a deacon called?

2 By what name is the *Promotor Fidei*, the official dealing juridically with processes of Beatification and Canonization better known?

3 In which medieval monastic centre of learning, in Normandy, had Lanfranc and St. Anselm been monks?

4 What did Queen Elizabeth II give Mother Teresa in the grounds of the Presidential Palace in New Delhi in November 1983?

5 Who was the Mellifluous Doctor?

6 The Books of the Chronicles, to translate their Hebrew title, in the Old Testament, are called in the Douay Bible by the Greek word for 'things left out' in the Vulgate. What is this word, Anglicised?

7 What is the name given to the military standard adopted by Constantine after his celebrated 'vision of light'. It was an adaptation of the existing Roman banner, but incorporating Christian symbols.

8 Which Irishman started a Shipping Company in Peru which expanded to an industrial conglomerate (still floating under his own name), was the first Catholic Mayor of New York, and a daily communicant?

9 What is the branch of theological science which pertains to the history or conduct of theological controversy?

10 Which early English Cistercian's treatise on Spiritual Friendship commences: 'When I was still just a lad at school, and the charm of my companions pleased me very much, I gave my whole soul to affection and devoted myself to love amid the ways and vices with which that age is wont to be threatened, so that nothing seemed to me more sweet, nothing more agreeable, nothing more practical than to love. And so, torn between conflicting loves and friendships, I was drawn now here, now there, and not knowing the law of true friendship, I was often deceived by its mere semblance'?

Q59

1. Who are the three angels mentioned by name in the Scriptures?

2. Which English Monsignor published, in 1928, a piece in *Essays in Satire* proving that Queen Victoria wrote *In Memoriam*?

3. How is the *Instituto per le Opera di Religione* vulgarly known?

4. What noun was Dr. Johnson defining in his dictionary when he wrote: 'The act of fuming with incense'?

5. Who wrote the hymn which starts with this verse:
   'Mother of Mercy, day by day,
   My love for thee grows more and more,
   Thy gifts are strewn upon my way
   Like sands upon the great seashore'?

6. Who played the parish priest in David Lean's 1970 film *Ryan's Daughter*?

7. For how long, to the half year, did Pope John XXIII reign?

8. From what disease did Job most likely suffer:
   Dysentry, Rabies, Leukaemia, Pellegra?

9. Which film maker defended his artistic subject matter by saying: 'I didn't write the Bible and I didn't invent sin'?

10. Of which saint is Phyllis McGinley writing:
    '- - - - - - was God's familiar. She often spoke
    To Him informally,
    As if together they shared some heavenly joke.
    Once, watching stormily
    Her heart's ambition wither to odds and ends,
    With all to start anew,
    She cried, "If this is the way You treat Your friends,
    No wonder You have so few!"
    There is no perfect record standing by
    Of God's reply'?

Q60

1 Name the conical mountain in County Mayo, Ireland, which is a traditional place of pilgrimage?

2 By what name were the lavatories in pre-Reformation monasteries known?

3 What is the liturgical book containing the chants of the Divine Office sung by cantors and choir?

4 What feast is held on the Thursday after Trinity Sunday?

5 When was the clerical tonsure abolished?

6 Who founded the Christian Brothers (Institute of the Brothers of the Christian Schools) and, indirectly, the Presentation Brothers?

7 Which French intellectual body was founded by Cardinal Richelieu in 1634, has included Racine, Voltaire, Chateaubriand and Victor Hugo, and flourishes today, with a membership limited to forty?

8 Which rite of the Mass begins with the absolution and vesting at the foot of the altar?

9 Which Cardinal claimed to be *non desideriis hominum, sed voluntate Dei*, Henry IX, King of Great Britain, France and Ireland?

10 Endogamy means marrying within one's religion (or tribe or social class etc). What word is its antonym?

Q 61

1   Which German Protestant theologian wrote, during World War II: 'Only he who shouts for the Jews may sing the Gregorian chant'?

2   Name the peoples who inhabited the land where a man who lived in tombs was used by the devils who possessed him to say their name was 'Legion'?

3   What was unusual about the election to the Papacy of the two late seventeenth century Popes, Clement X and Innocent XI?

4   What Mass vestment, from the Latin for 'a house', is worn over all the other vestments?

5   What is the name of the vessel used to show the Holy Eucharist during expositions, processions and benediction?

6   Which Queen of Sweden renounced Lutheranism, embraced Catholicism and abdicated her throne?

7   What kind of tree (all mainstream English translations are in accord) did Zaccheus climb to catch sight of Jesus?

8   Which twentieth century Catholic novelist took time from his biting satires to write a biography of St. Edmund Campion?

9   At which Office is the *Magnificat* recited or sung?

10 What word, a state of the after-life, is missing from this sentence of Jean Pierre Camus: 'If - - - - - - - - - is a species of hell as regards suffering, it is even more a species of paradise as regards heavenly love and sweetness'?

Q62

1 Which twentieth century British writer on Christian apologetics and of fantasy stories for children wrote: 'Culture is not everyone's road into Jerusalem, and for some it is the road out'?

2 Which Queen of Scotland has been canonised?

3 What apocalyptic event is missing from this line of Martin D'Arcy in *The Mind and Heart of Love*: 'Man is only wounded by the - - - - and therefore his high dignity remains'?

4 Where did Jesus tell Peter to find the half-shekel for the temple tax?

5 Who was responsible for the reform within the Cistercian Order at the Abbey of La Trappe in 1678?

6 What is the monthly publication containing the authentic and official Papal documents?

7 What aspect of the nomination of Giacomo Antonelli (1806–1876), Secretary of State to Pius IX, to the Cardinalate distinguished him from other Cardinals?

8 What was the association of Catholic laymen formed in the late eighteenth century to accept the House of Hanover and abandon Jacobite sympathies?

9 Which Roman church, aptly named, claims to hold the proclamation which Pilate ordered to be pinned to the cross?

10 What two types of monks did St. Benedict refer to as 'destestable' in his rule?

Q 63

1   Why is the Apostles Creed so called?

2   What is the motherhouse, and best known monastery, of the Carthusian Order?

3   What congregation of French Sisters were, until Vatican II, conspicuous by their butterfly headress?

4   Which monk, a naturalised American, wrote in *The Ascent to Truth*: 'The Church is not taught by theologians, they are taught by her. The Church is not sanctified by her saints, she sanctifies them with the Grace of Christ'?

5   Name the Latin hymn to the Holy Ghost, part of the liturgy of Pentecost, which is also widely used at solemn functions?

6   Where is the original monastery of St. Benedict?

7   In Canon Law what are 'subreption' and 'obreption'?

8   What, in Italy, are the Suburbicarian Dioceses?

9   What are the differences between an alb, a surplice and a rochet?

10 Where is Dante buried?

Q64

1 What was the nationality of Pope John XXI who, in 1276, died when the roof of the Papal study fell on his head:
Italian, Portuguese, French, Tunisian?

2 Which cleric was the subject of Aldous Huxley's 1941 study *Grey Eminence?*

3 To what was Dr. George Carey, the Church of England Primate and Archbishop of Canterbury, referring when he told an Anglican Synod: 'God has shown that what seems novel and risky is consonant with what has happened in the past'?

4 Provide the word missing from the following sentence concerning Mary Levison. A member of The Church of Scotland who was ordained in 1969, she was one of the Queen's chaplains in Scotland: 'A deep-seated taboo about pregnancy surfaced, which she dealt with by saying that those who were repelled by a pregnant woman preaching in the pulpit might have difficulty with - - - - - - , when the whole Church was expectant?

5 What is a *flabellum?*

6 What name is given to the climbing plant named after the suffering and death of Christ by the early South American missionaries, and why was it given?

7 Which French King was canonised?

8 What is the first article the priest puts on when vesting for Mass?

9 Which English Catholic apologist wrote, in 1901: 'Humility is the luxurious art of reducing ourselves to a point, not to a small thing or a large one, but to a thing with no size at all, so that to it all the cosmic things are what they really are, of immeasurable stature'?

10 Which Syrian saint (d. 373) whose name means 'Fruitful' was made a Doctor of the Church by Benedict XV? At the time that Pope said: 'This harp of the Holy Spirit never sings sweeter songs than when he has set his strings to sing the praises of Mary. A verse from one of his songs reads: God's Eden is Mary; in her is no tree of the knowledge of good and evil, no serpent that harms,

no Eve that kills, but from
her springs the Tree of Life
that restores the exiles to
Eden.'

Q65

1 'Folly to drink from
   puddles by the way
   When here at home the
   crystal fountains play.'
   These lines are translated
   from the German of a seventeenth century convert from
   Lutheranism, and priest,
   called Johannes Scheffler.
   He is better known by his
   confirmation name. What is
   it?

2 What term, possibly hurtful
   to U.S. citizens, did Leo XIII
   apply, in his Apostolic letter
   to Cardinal Gibbons of
   Baltimore in 1899, to the
   method of apologetics which
   stressed natural virtues to
   the neglect of dogmatic
   teaching, and spiritual direc-
   tion which preferred
   individual inspiration and
   the active virtues to external
   guidance and the passive
   virtues?

3 What is the difference
   between the altar breads as
   used in the Eastern, and the
   Western/Armenian
   Churches?

4 Which Dominican, called
   'The Great', was a teacher of
   St. Thomas Aquinas in Paris,
   recognised his genius and
   foretold his future greatness.
   He said when Aquinas died

that 'the light of the
Church' had been extin-
guished and, furthermore,
was himself proclaimed a
Doctor of the Church by
Pius XI?

5 What are the seven Spiritual
   Works of Mercy?

6 Who first used the term
   'Lamb of God' in direct
   reference to Christ?

7 What is the name of the
   grotto shrine near
   Motherwell in Scotland
   which is known as the
   'Scottish Lourdes' and
   attracts over 70,000 visitors a
   year?

8 Although an Abbess does
   not enjoy the jurisdiction of
   an Abbot what two symbols
   of rank is she entitled to
   use?

9 The following line is from
   Belloc's *Path to Rome*. What is
   the missing word: 'One's
   native place is the shell of
   one's soul, and one's - - - - - -
   is the kernel of that nut'?

10 Which office holder in the
    Roman Curia is, in effect,
    the Pope's Prime Minister?

Q 66

1   In what century did St. John of the Cross and St. Teresa of Avila live?

2   A German city's name means, literally, 'Monks'. Can you identify it?

3   What lay organization was founded in 1947 by Father Harold Colgan of Plainfield, New Jersey, when he survived a critical illness after invoking Our Lady of Fatima?

4   What is the circular band of white wool worn about the neck, with one pendant in front and one behind which the Pope confers upon Archbishops?

5   What is the distinction between a pagan and a heathen?

6   Who was the first Cardinal Archbishop of Westminster after the restoration of the English Hierarchy in 1850?

7   What are the eight hours of the monastic Office?

8   Two of the Beatitudes in St. Matthew's Gospel promise the same reward to the poor in spirit, and to those who suffer persecution for justice's sake. What is the reward?

9   From which French city did the Popes rule for most of the fourteenth century?

10 What was the family name of St. Bernadette, the visionary of Lourdes?

Q67

1 Who was the first native US citizen to be canonised?

2 What is the chalice-like vessel used to contain the Hosts on the altar, in the tabernacle and at Communion called?

3 Which French painter (1836–1902), given to representing the more carnal aspects of life in youth, underwent a form of conversion when in London painting *Christ appears to console two unfortunates in a ruin*, went to Palestine, and eventually produced 865 illustrations under the title *Le Vie de Notre Seigneur Jésus Christ*?

4 When was the right of sanctuary abolished in England?

5 What architectural feature, familiar to all later churches, was lacking in Norman places of worship?

6 Which sixteenth century Italian poet, celebrated in an eponymous play by Goethe ('a heightened *Werther*', he himself called the work) died the day before he was to be made the papal Poet Laureate?

7 What great and ancient hymn is, in addition to its liturgical use, sung in thanksgiving on special occasions?

8 Who wrote:
'Does the fish soar to find the ocean,
The eagle plunge to find the air,
That we ask the stars in motion
If they have rumour of Thee there'?

9 What do we call the square cap with three ridges formerly used by all clerics apart from Popes?

10 What Catholic Society, still very active world wide, was founded in 1833 by a twenty year old Sorbonne student, Frederic Ozaman?

Q68

1 What is the ceremony of sprinkling Holy Water lightly over the congregation at the beginning of High Mass called?

2 Which character in English drama became a nun, and was subsequently crucified over an anthill in Kinkanja?

3 In what year did Queen Elizabeth II make the first State Visit to the Vatican by a ruling British monarch: 1967, 1975, 1980, 1987?

4 In which Wagner opera does a Pope's staff bloom?

5 What is the missing word from this sentence of the Curé d'Ars: 'If we knew ourselves thoroughly, as God knows us, we could not live; we should die of - - - - - - '?

6 Is the title *Monsignor* bestowed on an individual cleric by the Vatican?

7 What town in the Holy Land is considered, by tradition, to have been the birthplace of St. John the Baptist?

8 What is the Curia office which used to be known as the Inquisition now called?

9 What were the eastern hermits who spent their lives on the tops of pillars known as?

10 'For where God hath a temple, the devil will have a chapel: where God hath sacrifices, the devil will have his oblations: where God hath ceremonies, the devil will have his traditions: where there is any religion, the devil will plant superstition: and 'tis a pitiful sight to behold and read what tortures, miseries it hath procured, what slaughter of souls it hath made ...' From what seventeenth century English divine, what sombre-titled work, and under what pseudonym did he first publish it?

Q69

1 Which Pope Pius died in captivity in Valence, France, in 1799?

2 What is, or perhaps was, the Order of Seraphim or Seraphic Order?

3 Of which political figure of the twentieth century do commentators suggest Nostradamus was speaking when he wrote as a prophecy: 'The great one who will be born of Verona and Vincenza who carries a very unworthy surname; he who at Venice will wish to take vengeance, himself taken by a man of the watch and sign'?

4 Which Irish playwright who, when asked on television in the 1960s whether he was not ashamed to be seen drunk on that medium, answered! 'Sure, I'm not at Mass when I'm on this thing, you know'?

5 What is the sixth Station of the Cross?

6 The Vatican employs 3,400 people. How many of these are lay:
   900, 1,570, 2,600, 3,100?

7 Which two saints, blood brothers, are known as *The Apostles of the Slavs*. They are co-patrons of Europe with St. Benedict.

8 What Christian concept is feminine in Hebrew, neuter in Greek and masculine in Latin?

9 Which saint, the patron of invalids, is generally depicted with a dog?

10 Who wore white wool to Jerusalem?

Q70

1 Which notable nineteenth century convert wrote in his spiritual autobiography: 'I understood that ... nature was a parable, scripture was an allegory, pagan literature, philosophy and mythology, properly understood, were but a preparation for the gospel'?

2 What is the rule book for the *Opus Dei* movement called?

3 Which Marian shrine in Ireland has its own airport?

4 The full title of a particular Eastern Patriarch is as follows: 'His Holiness the Lord (name of incumbent), Patriatch of - - - - - - - , the Great City of God, of Cilicia, of Iberia, of Syria, of Arabia, and of all the East, Father of Fathers, Pastor of Pastors, Thirteenth Apostle' What is the city?

5 Which great Anglican poet, according to Aubrey's *Brief Lives*: 'Also writt a folio in Latin which, because the parson of Hitcham could not read, his widow condemned to the uses of good housewifry'?

6 What word (it has passed into English) did Jephtha make the men at the Jordan fords pronounce to distinguish those from Ephraim from the Gilead allies? (The Ephraimites pronounced it as 'S' instead of 'SH' and were killed on the spot.)

7 When Pope Clement XIV suppressed the Jesuits in 1773 only two Monarchs refused to recognise the Brief. Neither was Roman Catholic. Who were they?

8 Which two Popes occupied the Chair of Peter between 1846 and 1903?

9 Why are a priest's hands covered when he blesses with the monstrance?

10 Which twentieth century Bavarian stigmatic and visionary reported: 'Then the executioners put something like a staff in the hands of our dear Saviour, ... they now amuse themselves with it, making mock genuflexions before Him. I was especially indignant about the contempt implied by this bowing of the knee before Our Saviour. They spit in His face and give themselves up to uncontrollable laughter ... Our Saviour often opens His mouth as if to get more air, and as if He is thirsty. At this

one of them spits directly
into His mouth; this form of
insult deeply grieves Our
Divine Saviour'?

Q71

1   Which saint whose blood is kept in a phial and said to liquefy and bubble up to eighteen times a year when placed near a silver bust believed to contain his head, is the patron of Naples?

2   Though the word 'Pope' derives from the Greek for 'father' from where do we take the word 'Pontiff'?

3   Did Judas leave the Last Supper before or after the washing of the feet?

4   Which Liberal Democrat M.P. for Mosely Hill, Liverpool, during the 1980s was leading voice in the anti-abortionist lobby at that time?

5   Who was the last Roman Catholic cleric to be executed at Tyburn?

6   The Vatican intends to build a new observatory on Mt. Graham in Arizona, USA. Where is the present one?

7   Which seventeenth century thinker, author of *Pensees*, wrote: 'Philosophers astonish ordinary men; Christians astonish philosophers'?

8   In which book of the Bible do we find a girl called Rhoda?

9   What is an assistant Bishop to a Diocesan Bishop, with a right to succession to the See known as?

10 Which canonised Catalonian Jesuit went to Columbia in 1610 and devoted the rest of the thirty-three years of his life to caring for the African slaves and called himself 'the slave of the negroes forever'?

Q72

1   Which Irish Archbishop of Armagh founded Mellifont, the first Cistercian Abbey in Ireland? He died at Clairvaux in the arms of his friend and biographer St. Bernard.

2   With reference to the preceding question prophecies contained in a document of 1590, attributed to the saint, foretell the lives of the Popes. There are only two more to be fulfilled. After John Paul II the prophecy says *Gloria Olivae* which commentators suggest may mean a Benedictine, as the Benedictines are also known as Olivetans. The last prophecy actually gives a name. What is it?

3   In the House that Jack built, what woke the priest all shaven and shorn?

4   What liturgical rite is used by the Copts of Egypt and Ethiopia?

5   Of which South African-born poet, and translator of the Poems of St. John of the Cross, did Edith Sitwell write: 'This simple giant ... was the true knight of Our Lady, and if he had to be taken by death, it was suitable that this should have

been when he was returning from the celebration of her Son's Resurrection ... He died as he had lived, like a flash of lightning'?

6   What word literally means: 'one taught by word of mouth'?

7   In the *Oxyrhynchus Papyri* discovered early in the twentieth century are the words: 'Lift up the stones and there thou shalt find me; cleave to the wood and I am there.' To whom are the words attributed?

8   This twenty-three word sentence by Meister Eckhart has been rearranged alphabetically. Set it right.
    because cannot for give God He He help His I it; it is loving me, nature never no or thanks to whether would

9   In Germany in the first half of the second millenium, what were the terms used for those who: a) favoured the Emperors in their relations to the Papacy; and b) favoured the Papacy in relation to the Temporal Powers?

10 Which nineteenth century Italian Republican wrote that the Church was

doomed 'because it has
betrayed its mission to
protect the weak, because
for three centuries and a
half it has committed fornication with the Princes of
this world, because at the
bidding of every unbelieving
Government it has crucified
Jesus afresh in the name of
egoism'?

Q73

1 What form of address is used to respond to the Holy Father on formal occasions and in documents?

2 Who was the only Pope to voluntarily resign office?

3 By what single word are the Ten Commandments known?

4 Name the Spanish city where there is an English seminary?

5 What is the Cathedral of the See of Rome, containing the seat of the Pope in his office as Bishop of Rome?

6 For much of the second half of the twentieth century who has been the (to English speakers, unfortunately named) Cardinal Archbishop of Manila, in the Philippines?

7 The cause for the canonization of the great, great grand-uncle of the Princess of Wales has been introduced. Who was he?

8 What is the name of the estimable, largely youth orientated, ecumenical community in Burgundy, France?

9 What is the one word missing from this sentence from St. Augustine: 'We do not praise in - - - - - - - the fact that they are - - - - - - - but that they are - - - - - - - dedicated to God in Holy Chastity'?

10 When British homosexual Catholics, who had no wish to leave the Church yet felt that the Church shunned them, organised themselves into a pressure group, what name did they adopt?

Q74

1   The Council of Ephesus (431) used a term other than *Mater Dei* to identify Our Lady. What was it?

2   When was the Feast of Christ the King instituted: 1894, 1908, 1924, 1945?

3   What inter-racial body does the acronym WAAC represent to London's Catholics?

4   What is the fragrant oil from the root of the small herbaceous plant *Nardostachys Jasamansi*, used to anoint the feet of Jesus at Bethany, better known as?

5   Apart from letters from the Pope what did Marco Polo and his uncles present to Kublai Khan at Peking in 1275:
    Oil from the lamp at the Holy Sepulchre,
    A splinter of the True Cross,
    A gold reliquary,
    A copy of the Vulgate?

6   What word designates a Bishop who has authority, not only over the Bishops of his own province, but over several provinces and Metropolitans?

7   What spiritual doctrine of self-annihilation was condemned by Innocent XI in 1687 though many religious thinkers flirted with it?

8   What was the name given to the early seventeenth century Jesuit missions of Paraguay which endeavoured to convert the Indians by spiritual means?

9   Of which great English literary light did Archdeacon Davies, an Anglican clergyman of Gloucester, write in a biography in the late seventeenth century 'He died a papyst'?

10 Which Franciscan saint's *Life of Christ* contains these lines on the Nativity: 'And what one among them (the angels) having received the gladsome news, could have remained in heaven, nor descend obsequiously to visit their Lord thus humbled, thus reduced to the lowest condition upon earth? None of them could be capable of so great an arrogance ... This to me is a most pleasing subject of meditation, whether it happened exactly as here related or not'?

Q75

1 Who wrote of St. Alphonsus Rodriquez, a Jesuit lay-brother in the Balearic Islands:

    'Yet God (that hews mountain and continent,
    Earth, all, out; who with trickling increment
    Veins violets and tall trees makes more and more)
    Could crowd career with conquest while there went
    Those years and years by of world without event
    That in Majorca Alfonso watched the door'?

2 What is the small case in which the Sacred Host is preserved or carried called?

3 What was the language of the people in Palestine in Jesus' time?

4 Which English Benedictine monk lived in a Southern Indian ashram from the 1950s until his death in the '90s and interpreted the *Gita* in a Christian context?

5 Is the celibacy of Catholic clergy a matter of doctrine or discipline?

6 How is a Cardinal formally addressed?

7 What doctrine did the Pope declare as an Article of Faith on the 8th December 1854?

8 Who is the patroness of Paris?

9 What seventeenth century movement denied, or at least questioned, Grace and Free Will?

10 What was the stream that Christ crossed to enter the Garden of Gethsemane?

Q76

1 Who said; 'Give me an army saying the Rosary and I will conquer the world'?

2 What Act, called 'the whip with six strings' by Protestants, did Henry VIII push through Parliament in 1539 which reaffirmed transubstantiation, auricular confession, communion in one kind, clerical celibacy, and provided the death penalty for the denial of these doctrines?

3 By what other name do we know the Canticle of the Blessed Virgin?

4 What word used to be used to designate a person who travelled to sell or distribute religious books?

5 What is the missing word from the following epigram on the Bible:

'Men ope this book, their favourite - - - - - in mind;
Each seeks his own, and each his own does find.'?

6 What were the gravediggers in the catacombs called?

7 What is the name of the Biblical Canon, presumably compiled in Rome around 180 AD, which contrasts surveys of the Scriptures as well as historical and other information from which the following is an extract: 'When his fellow disciples exhorted him (John) he said, "Fast with me for three days from today, and then let us relate to each other whatever may be revealed to each of us". On the same night it was revealed to Andrew that John should relate all things in his own name as they remembered them'?

8 What is the (rather charming) name for the last pre-Reformation Cistercian Abbey to be built in Scotland?

9 Who designed and inaugurated Vatican Radio in 1931 and supervised it until his death in 1937?

10 Which famous French parish priest said: 'God might have created a more beautiful world, but he could not have given life to a creature more beautiful than Mary'?

Q77

1   What is the meaning of the Latin word *cathedra* from which we get 'Cathedral'?

2   In which country is Trent, where the General Council was held from 1545–63?

3   What was the married name of Evelyn Underhill (1875–1941), authoress of *Mysticism; Concerning the Inner Life* and *The Golden Sequence* etc.?

4   Who were the parents of St. John the Baptist?

5   Which Order is called 'The White Friars'?

6   Who founded the Y.M.C.A. in London in 1844?

7   Why did Don Bosco call his congregation of teaching brothers 'Salesians'?

8   Which Scottish Jesuit whose mission, as he put it, was to 'unteach heresy', was hanged on 28th February 1615 at Glasgow Cross?

9   Which Pope died on September 28th 1978?

10 Why was a fish the symbol of early Christianity?

Q78

1 Which fourteenth century English priest who espoused predestination, denied transubtantiation and preached a fiery anti-clericalism, had his bones dug up and burned, by order of the Council of Constance, forty-three years after his death: John Wyclif, William Langland, John Gower, Ranulph Higden?

2 Why does Rome require Anglican clergy to be ordained in the Roman rite when they desire to exercise priesthood as Roman Catholics?

3 Between the Reformation and the Catholic Emancipation Act what word was used of a person who refused to submit to the Act of Uniformity and to take the oath of allegiance to the Monarch as the supreme head of the Church of England?

4 The election of Benedict XIV in 1740 took six months. How many times did the Cardinals vote before the choice was made: 192, 242, 255, 328?

5 How many episcopal areas are there in the Diocese of Westminster?

6 What, in eighteenth century demotic Irish, was Saint Monday?

7 Who was the King of Salem, mentioned in the Mass, met by Abraham after his expedition against the Four Kings? The King of Salem gave him bread and wine, and he gave the King of Salem a tenth of the booty.

8 What former alcoholic collapsed and died in a Dublin Street on Trinity Sunday 1925 and was declared Venerable fifty years later?

9 Who was the Jesuit Missionary to China who was the subject of Vincent Cronin's 1955 study *The Wise Man from the West*?

10 What word is missing from this sentence of St. Augustine: 'The spiritual virtue of a - - - - - - - - - is like light; although it passes among the impure it is not polluted'?

Q 79

1 What is the name of the liturgical vestment composed of strips of material from two to four inches wide and about eighty inches long, with a cross in the centre which is kissed by the priest before being placed over the shoulders?

2 What doctrine teaches that nothing in the universe is real save the ineffable, super-cosmic One, and that all in space, time and finite experience is mere appearance?

3 ' "How in Tartarus," cried Flambeau, "did you ever hear of the spiked bracelet?" "Oh, one's little flock, you know," said - - - - - - - - - - - .' Who?

4 What nationality was St. Peter Canisius?

5 What form of music is used in the singing of the Divine Office in monasteries, cathedrals etc.?

6 What is the derivation of the word 'chapel'?

7 'A man walks upright, and the food of his body is shut as if in a well-made purse. When the time of his necessity comes, the purse is opened and then shut again, in most seemly fashion. And it is God who does this, as it is shown when he says that He comes down to us in our humblest needs. For He does not despise what He has made, nor does He disdain to serve us in the simplest natural functions of our body, for the love of the soul which He created in His own likeness.' From the quill of which English authoress?

8 What is the branch of theology which investigates and expresses the true sense of Scripture?

9 What was the religious affiliation of George I?

10 What word is missing from this sentence of Oscar Wilde in *De Profundis*: 'He who is in a state of - - - - - - - - - cannot receive grace ... for in life as in art the mood of - - - - - - - - - closes up the channels of the soul, and shuts out the airs of heaven'?

Q80

1 In 1640 a book by Cornelius Jansen was published posthumously which gave rise to the errors of Jansenism and was officially condemned by the Church. What was the title of the book?

2 What is the ecclesiastical standing of the Archbishop of Dublin: Prefect Apostolic, Exarch, Closet Cardinal, Primate of Ireland?

3 Who was the shepherd of Tekoa?

4 Which Protestant Canon of Durham, in his *Journal of a Tour of Italy in 1850* was, in Ronald Knox's words in *The Man Who tried to Convert the Pope*, 'Off to Rome with the Keys of the Vatican in his pocket'?

5 What is the Catholic British ministry to Merchant Seamen called?

6 What is *Caesaropapism*?

7 What is the Aramaic word for 'skull'?

8 What is the missing word from a statement by Cardinal John O'Connor, Archbishop of New York: 'The Church is an unapologetically hierarchal organisation, hierarchal because it is - - - - - - - - -'?

9 Which two early Popes, both saints, are linked together in the martyrologies and share a feast day, yet weren't even contemporaries: Pius and Victor, Gaius and Soter, Felix and Sixtus, Urban and Fabian?

10 Which poet, clergyman, former teacher and correspondent of Gerald Manley Hopkins wrote these lines:
'For though the soul pants with fierce ecstasy
The unattainable to grasp, to be
For ever mingled with infinity;
And this is vain, since God himself withdraws
From human knowledge, e'en as its own laws
Seclude the soul from sense;
Yet not from love He hies;
From love God never flies'?

Q81

1   What are the six sins against the Holy Spirit?

2   Name the Irish Cistercian monastery with a reputation for caring for alcoholics?

3   Who was the architect of the unfinished *Sagrada Familia* church in Barcelona?

4   What prayer did Margaret Thatcher recite outside number 10 Downing Street in 1979?

5   What are, or were, 'Minims'?

6   Which psalm is the prayer *Miserere?*

7   It is said that St. Maurilius instituted the Feast of the Nativity of the Blessed Virgin in 430 because a parishioner heard the angels singing in heaven and, on asking the reason, was told that they were rejoicing on that night because it was Mary's birthday. What was the date?

8   Name the seven churches of the Apocalypse.

9   Only one Catholic Church in Moscow remained open through the Communist period. It is in the Mala Lubyanka. To which saint is it dedicated?

10 What is the missing word from this sentence of Schopenhauer: 'The doctor views mankind in all its weaknesses; the lawyer in all its wickedness; the theologian in all its - - - - - - - - -'?

Q 82

1   What collective name is given to the first five books of the Old Testament?

2   Who founded the Carthusian Order?

3   Where is John Duns Scotus, the thirteenth century Scottish Franciscan theologian, buried?

4   Who received sixteen revelations, or Shewings, on the 13th May 1373?

5   Who was the first person from the American continent to be canonised?

6   Name the seven deadly sins.

7   Who was the only English Pope?

8   Why was the Geneva Bible known as the 'Breechers Bible'?

9   In which US Cistercian monastery was Thomas Merton a monk?

10   Which great English poet wrote the following: 'I am not of the opinion to think the Church a vine ... because she cannot subsist without clasping about the elm of worldly strength and felicity, as if the heavenly city could not support itself without the props and buttresses of secular authority. They extol Constantine because he extolled them; as our home-bred monks in their histories blanch the kings their benefactors, and brand those that went about to be their correctors. If he had curbed the growing pride, avarice and luxury of the clergy, then every page of his story would have swelled with his faults, and that which Zozimus the heathen writes of him would have come in to boot'? (As a clue, when he was born *Timon of Athens* was playing to packed houses in Southwark, and on the Continent Francis de Sales was preparing to publish his *Introduction to the Devout Life.*)

Q83

1   What virtue has been defined as: 'That quality of spirit which is marked by peaceable temper, gentleness, self-respect without vanity, and patient submission to injury and offence without resentfulness and retaliation. It connotes, not feebleness of will or easy compliance with wrongdoing, but rather that firm and constant mastery of oneself under provocation which springs from calm and trustful surrender to God's will and which accepts hard and perplexing experiences as a part of the discipline of the Christian life'?

2   What liturgical vestment is a semi-circular piece of cloth worn over the shoulders and fastened at the breast with a clasp?

3   Which Irish border lake holds three-day pilgrimages on one of its islands and is considered to be one of the most arduous pilgrimages in the world?

4   Which fourteenth century Religious did Pope John XXIII designate as the patron of advertising?

5   In May 1995 Pope John Paul II canonised two local saints in the Czech Republic. One was St. Zdislave of Lembreck. Who was the other?

6   What is the name given to the central part of the Mass, which comes after the Offertory and before the Communion?

7   Which nineteenth century writer said the following – in a speech at Glasgow University – of Pope Nicholas V (1397–1455), the Pontiff whose love of letters led to his founding the Vatican Library: 'No department of literature owes so much to him as history. By him were introduced to the knowledge of Western Europe two great and unrivalled models of historical composition, the work of Herodotus and the work of Thucydides. By him, too, our ancestors were first made acquainted with the graceful and lucid simplicity of Xenophon and with the manly good sense of Polybius.'?

8   Which renegade Anglican priest, author of *Narrative of the Horrid Plot and Conspiracy of the Popish Party* (1679); *The*

*Cabinet of Jesuit's Secrets
Opened, issued and completed
by a Gentleman of quality*
(1769); *The Pope's Warehouse,
or The Merchandise of the
Whore of Rome* (1769); *The
Witch of Endor, or the
Witchcrafts of the Roman
Jezebel, in which you have an
account of the Exorcisms or
Conjurations of the Papists*
(1679), was, despite such a
flurry of mock-Nationist
activity in 1679, fined
£100,000 on 18th June 1682
by Judge Jeffries, who said of
him: 'He deserves more
punishment than the law of
the land can inflict.'?

9   How many men were killed
    when the Tower of Silo fell
    on them?

10 What is defined as: 'A
    musical composition for solo
    voices, chorus, orchestra
    and organ, to a religious
    text generally taken from
    Holy Scripture.'?

Q84

1 Name the nine orders of angels.

2 Which congregation of Religious women was founded by St. Francis de Sales and St. Jane Frances de Chantal in 1610?

3 Who do historians reckon was the first Pope to assume a name other than his own on ascending to the Papacy: St. Leo the Great, Felix II, St. Silverius; John II?

4 List the seven Corporal Works of Mercy.

5 By what treaty was the Vatican City State created in 1929?

6 What Italian word, used by Pope John XXIII to sum up the need and idea for Vatican II, has passed into the English language as descriptive of the process of reform and renewal in the Church?

7 A familiar three-word expression is missing from this statement by Franz Kafka: 'Only our concept of Time makes it possible for us to speak of the --- -- -------- by that name; in reality it is a summary court in perpetual session.'

8 Where was the first Roman Catholic church to be consecrated in England after the Reformation?

9 What name is given to a university which has been canonically erected and which is authorised by the *Sacred Congregation for Catholic Education* to confer degrees in specific fields of study?

10 Which fourteenth century English mystic wrote, in *The Ladder of Perfection*: 'For you can be certain that though you may watch and fast, use the scourge and do all that you can, you will never acquire purity and chastity except by the help of God and His grace of humility. Indeed, you might kill yourself before you could destroy your sinful inclinations and feeling in mind or body by physical penance. But by the grace of Jesus working in a humble soul the roots of sin can be cut and destroyed, and its source dried up. And this is true chastity of body and soul.'?

Q85

1. Name the world-wide religious brotherhood which took its origins from the spiritual inspiration of Charles de Foucauld and was given existence by Père René Voillaume?

2. Which famous work of art, which is twenty-nine feet wide and fifteen feet high, covers the wall of the refectory of the Dominican convent of Holy Mary of the Graces in Milan?

3. After the Ascension of Our Lord, who was chosen by lot to make up the Twelve in place of Judas Iscariot?

4. Who was the first citizen of the United States to be canonized?

5. In what year is the centenary of the death of St. Térèse of Lisieux?

6. Name the hymn canticle of the Mass which is omitted during Advent, Lent and at funerals.

7. What is the heresy that teaches that Christ was not the Son of God at birth, but only became so through St. John's baptism in the Jordan?

8. What is the incense-burning vessel used during solemn liturgies called?

9. A Hebrew word meaning 'to strengthen' or 'confirm' is used by Christ twenty-eight times in St. Matthew's Gospel and, in its doubled form, twenty-six times in St. John's. What is it?

10. From whose translation of which spiritual classic is the following an extract: 'We could have peace to our hearts' content, if only we would not concern ourselves with the things other people are saying or doing, things which are no business of ours. How can a man expect to have lasting peace when he is always minding other people's business, always looking out for the chance of engaging in other peoples activities, so that recollection is only possible in a small degree, or at rare intervals? Blessed are the simple; they shall have peace to their hearts' content.'?

Q86

1 What is a vernicle?

2 What term is employed in the act of excommunication?

3 When was the obligation of celibacy first imposed on clerics by a Church Council?

4 Name the Catholic mother and anti-contraception campaigner who lost a case against an early 1980s High Court ruling that doctors could supply contraceptive pills to girls under sixteen without their parents consent?

5 In what year was the song *Amazing Grace* top of the hit parade:
1968, 1970, 1972, 1974?

6 One hour before the conclave which elected Angelo Roncalli to the Papal Throne as John XXIII (28th October 1958) one of the Sacred College, Cardinal Mooney, died. Where was Cardinal Mooney's See?

7 The following is clause fourteen of the Edict of Nantes (1578): 'The practice of this religion is forbidden in our court and suite, in our dominions beyond the mountains, in our city of Paris, or within five leagues thereof.' Against which body was it directed?

8 On how many occasions in the Gospels is the Blessed Virgin recorded as having spoken directly?

9 From which book of major world influence is the following taken: 'They declared, "We have put to death the Messiah Jesus the Son of Mary ..." They did not kill him; he was made to resemble another for them.'?

10 The second Archbishop of Canterbury who, according to Bede the Venerable, when discouraged by the undoing of St. Augustine's work and was preparing to flee to Gaul, met St. Peter in a vision who scolded him for deserting his flock and whipped him soundly. What was his name?

Q87

1. By what self-effacing, if somewhat bizarre, name is a contemporary visionary in Australia known?
2. What word from the Greek *oikos* meaning 'house', gave rise to a verb meaning 'to inhabit', which generated a noun meaning 'the inhabited world', which prompted another to encompass 'the whole world', which the Latin borrowed to mean the same thing and we borrowed from the Latin and use in a religious context?
3. Which notable Church of Scotland minister, later ennobled, rebuilt the Abbey of Iona and founded the Iona Community?
4. Which European country, with no official religion, has a television station owned by the Catholic Church?
5. Which Central American Archbishop was shot while saying Mass in 1980?
6. Who did St. Paul leave ill in Miletus?
7. Which member of the British Royal family flew to Rome in 1992 with the sole purpose of meeting Mother Teresa of Calcutta?
8. 'Even if - - - - - - - - - - - - - repents and becomes the most pius man of our time, it is incumbent on - - - - - - - - - - - - to employ everything he has, his life and his wealth, to send him to hell.' Who said it, of whom, to whom?
9. How many letters by St. Paul are in the New Testament?
10. 'A cold coming we had of it,
    Just the worst time of the year
    For a journey, and such a long journey'
    Who was making the journey in this T.S. Eliot poem?

Q88

1   Name the third century sect, which flourished in Arabia, was converted by Origen and believed that the soul perished with the body but that both would be resurrected on the day of Judgement. This heresy was based on St. Paul's *First Letter to Timothy* (6:16): 'God, *who only hath immortality*' which they interpreted as ascribing undying life to God alone, thereby precluding its unbroken possession by man.

2   What is the 'second death' spoken of in *The Apocalypse*? (21:8)

3   By what name is Agnes Bojaxhin better known?

4   When did Rome cease to prescribe abstinence from the eating of meat as the universal manner for the observance of the fast on Fridays?

5   What Monastic Order, there was only one, originated in England?

6   Which British born saint is the patron of Germany?

7   Which Scottish Christian name means 'disciple of Columb'?

8   By what action is a Pope officially pronounced dead?

9   What is the word given to the shaving of the head of a monk or a cleric to signify his withdrawal from the vanities of the world?

10   What, and when, were the Rogation Days?

Q89

1 What was unconventional about Caravaggio's representation of Christ in his painting *Supper at Emmaus?*

2 Possibly the best known of the early heresies taught that the Son of God was a creature of similar, but not the same substance as the Father. What is the heresy called?

3 How many chapters are there in the Book of Isaiah: 46, 55, 66, 75?

4 Which seventh century English saint, Abbot of Malmesbury and Bishop of Sherborne, was the first English scholar of distinction and of whose austerities it is recorded that he was wont to recite the entire psalter standing up to his neck in ice-cold water? The cape in Dorset usually called St. Alban's head is misnamed after him.

5 Which valley, some eleven miles from Jerusalem, do some people believe has been ear-marked for the site of the Last Judgement?

6 What is bination?

7 Which unlikely American actress portrayed the Virgin Mary in the 1943 Twentieth Century Fox film on the Lourdes apparitions, *The Song of Bernadette?*

8 Who is the best known member, though very little is known about him, of the quasi-monastic order of brotherhoods and sisterhoods founded in the fourteenth century by Gerard Groote and known as 'The Brethren of the Common Life'?

9 Which eleventh century Queen of Bavaria walked unscathed on plough-shares and, together with her husband, King Henry, has been canonized?

10 Which Dutchman, a friend of St. Thomas More, wrote: 'If what has been commanded be not in the power of one, all the numberless exhortations of the Scriptures, and also all the promises, threatenings, expostulations, reproofs, asseverations, benedictions and maledictions, together with all forms of precepts, must of necessity stand coldly useless'?

Q 90

1   Wolfgang Amadeus Mozart had two other Christian names, after a great Doctor of the Eastern Church. What were they?

2   Which Doctor of the Church wrote: 'As to the fable that there are antipodes, that is to say, men on the opposite side of the earth, where the sun rises when it sets on us, men who walk with their feet opposite ours, there is no reason for believing it'?

3   What do we call compositions which profess to have been written by Biblical personages, but are not accepted as part of the Biblical canon?

4   Who was the Roman Emperor during Jesus' life time?

5   What is the branch of theology which deals with the defence and proof of Christianity?

6   In Shakespeare's *Henry VIII*, Act 5 Scene 3, the King asks Cranmer to be godfather to the infant Elizabeth. Cranmer demurs, saying that he is poor and the King answers: 'Come, come, my Lord. You'd spare your spoons?' To what spoons does he refer?

7   What were John Paul I's Christian name and surname?

8   Who wrote, in French, on the 24th April 1916, at Dunkirk: 'To live the cosmic life is to be dominated by the consciousness that one is an atom in the body of the mystical and cosmic Christ. The man who so lives dismisses as irrelevant a host of preoccupations that absorb the interests of other men; his life is projected further, and his heart more widely receptive. There you have my intellectual testament'?

9   Which prominent Catholic theologian was deprived of his licence to teach theology by the Church in 1981?

10 Of which Monarch did Lytton Stratchey write in *Elizabeth and Essex*: 'A sacred candle was lighted and put into his hand, the flame, as he clutched it closer and closer, casting lurid shadows upon his face; and so, in ecstasy and in torment, in absurdity and in greatness, happy, miserable, horrible, and holy, - - - - - - - - - - went off to meet the Trinity'?

Q91

1 In the debate over clerical celibacy what does the acronym MOMM represent?

2 What fourth century Roman martyr buried on the Aurelian Way, and about whom nothing else is known, gave his name to an area of central London?

3 What is the origin of the much-used monogram I.H.S.?

4 To what Religious Order did Erasmus belong?

5 Which of Europe's Cathedral's was started in 1386 and completed under Napoleon in 1805?

6 Who set William Blake's poem *Jerusalem* to music in 1915?

7 Are women eligible for Papal knighthoods?

8 What are the missing words from William Johnson's *Being in Love; The Practice of Christian Prayer* 1988:
   'God is light in Himself, but - - - - - - - - to us.
   God is all in Himself, but - - - - - - - to us.
   God is fullness in Himself, but - - - - to us'?

9 What is the Vatican post of 'Master of the Sacred Palace' and members of what Order have tradition-ally held it?

10 Who, in the Gospels, was the brother of St. Andrew?

Q 92

1 In what year was the new *Codex Juris Canonici* instituted:
   1923, 1961, 1970, 1983?

2 Who coined the term 'Anti-Christ'?

3 When was the 'Index' of books prohibited to Catholics first launched:
   1512, 1534, 1569, 1571?

4 Name the Act of Parliament, passed in 1664 and repealed in 1812, which made it an offence for more than four persons over sixteen to attend services 'in other manner than is allowed by the (Church of England) liturgy'?

5 In which British city did Pope John Paul II end his 1983 tour?

6 In which decade of the twentieth century did Peron disestablish the Catholic Church in Argentina?

7 The following words of Pope Paul VI are written on a plaque in the crypt of Our Lady of Grace church, near *San Giovani Rotundo*, Italy. To whom do they refer: 'Because he was a philosopher? A scholar? Wealthy? No. Because he said Mass humbly, confessing morning to night, and was representative, stamped, of the stigmata of Our Lord. He was a man of prayer and suffering'?

8 William Beckford visited the great twelth century Portuguese Cistercian monastery at Alcobaça in 1835. Of its kitchens he wrote: 'The most distinguished temple of - - - - - - - - in all Europe.' What is the (hopefully inappropriate) missing word?

9 What term is used in the study of theories of how the universe came into being?

10 Account for the following bill:
   To God 2 shillings &
   8 pence
   Pilate and his wife
   2 shillings
   Devil and Judas 1 shilling
   & 6 pence
   Fauston for cock-croying
   7 pence
   Fauston for hanging Judas
   5 pence

Q 93

1 Which Brazilian theologian and author of sixty-seven books resigned from his Order and from the Priesthood in 1992 saying that: 'Freedom of communication has been practically withdrawn from me within the formal structures of the Church. I consider that to censor in advance everything I write ... is abusive and contrary to the sense of Canon Law. One cannot breathe without air, one cannot create without freedom.'?

2 What name is given to the nine day devotion for some specific purpose?

3 In the dialogue between Canterbury and Rome what does the acronym A.R.C.I.C. represent?

4 Who was the last Roman Catholic Monarch of England?

5 Who cut off a pig's trotter to feed a sick brother and incurred the wrath of the swineherd?

6 The Church of Lyons, founded in 150 AD is the oldest Church in Christendom after Rome and the senior See of France. What honorific title is attached to its Archbishopric?

7 Name the five Joyful Mysteries of the Rosary.

8 When is *Laetare* Sunday?

9 What is the missing word from this extract from one of St. John Chrysostom's homilies: 'It is a journey for a season; a sleep longer than usual. If thou fearest - - - - -, thou should also fear sleep.'?

10 Who founded the (English) *Tablet*, the weekly Catholic newspaper in 1840?

Q94

1 What is the distinction between the Ultramontane and the Gallican schools of theological thought?

2 Has Rome always acknowledged the validity of the Orthodox Churches' priestly orders?

3 What was the name of the former chairman of the *Banco Ambrosiano*, known as 'God's Banker', who was found hanging from scaffolding beneath Blackfriars Bridge, London, in June 1982?

4 'Lord give us a good digestion, and something good to digest.' This was the beginning of a canonized English statesman's Grace Before Meals. Who was he?

5 What is the difference between 'calced' and 'discalced' Religious?

6 Which saint's canonization in 1950 was attended by her murderer?

7 Which saints, none of whom are known by name, and none of whom had ever heard of Christ, have a canonical feast day?

8 What is the first question and answer in the Penny Catechism?

9 By what name was the cup used by Jesus at the Last known in medieval legends?

10 Which Pope proclaimed in an encyclical, in 1929, that co-education was contrary to all Catholic principles?

Q 95

1 What marks distinguish Grunewald's crucifixion and entombment paintings from similar scenes by other noted artists?

2 What was Knownothingism?

3 What, according to tradition, were the names of Our Lady's parents?

4 The present Turkish city of Koyna, famous for its Whirling Dervishes, was visited by St. Paul and St. Barnabas according to the Acts of the Apostles. What was it called then?

5 In the world of religious publishing what does S.P.C.K. stand for?

6 Which Pope, who had been married before he received Orders, had a son who was also Pope?

7 In Jean-François Millet's famous painting *The Angelus* in the Louvre, what have the peasants been digging in the field when they pause to pray?

8 What are the Mechitarists?

9 What city is the religious capital of Ireland?

10 What two words (initials are provided) are missing from this quote from Proclus of Constantinople in his *Encomium on the All-Holy*

Mary, Mother of God: 'She is the awe-inspiring loom of the Incarnation, wherein, in a way unspeakable, was woven the garment of the H - - - - - - - - - U - - - - , with the Holy Spirit as weaver; the overshadowing power from above, the connecting thread; the ancient fleece of Adam, the wool; the unde-filed flesh from the Virgin, the threaded woof; the shuttle, the immeasurable grace of her who bore, with the Logos as Artist ...'?

Q 96

1 What Mexican shrine attracts 10,000 visitors each year?

2 Who were the Acoemetae?

3 The authenticity of which piece of handwoven material was discredited by carbon dating in October 1988?

4 The remains of which Biblical trio are said to be in three gold caskets behind the main altar of Cologne Cathedral?

5 Who published, in 1923, a Treatise on Ascetical and Mystical Theology called *The Spiritual Life*, which has become the text book of seminaries and novitiates throughout the Catholic World?

6 Who is the patron saint of Maastricht, whose bones are kept in a church dedicated to him and taken through the city in times of trouble?

7 Name the European city having the first church to be dedicated to the Sacred Heart.

8 A sixteenth century Dutchman who became a Jesuit, and was canonized in 1925, was born Peter de Hondt, a family name that means 'of the dog'. How was it Latinised?

9 Which nineteenth/twentieth century English poetess wrote:
    'None can be like Him, none!
    In love? In grief? Nay, man's capacity,
    Rifled unto its depths, is reached, is done –
    Christ's an unfathomable sea.
    None can be like Him, none;
    Not she who bore him. Yet I saw the whole
    Eternal, infinite Christ within the one
    Small mirror of her soul'?

10 What is the missing word from Robert Hugh Benson's *Come Rack! Come Rope!*:
    '- - - - is a disease that must be borne with patience! Time, indeed, will cure it; yet, until the cure is complete, elders must bear it as well as they can, and not seem to pay too much attention to it. A rigorous and prudent diet, long hours of sleep, plenty of occupation – these are the remedies for the fever!'?

Q97

1 Although not the first or last episode in the sorry story of the schism between the Eastern and Western Churches, what year, coinciding with the ugly arguments between the Patriarch Michael Cerularius and Cardinal Humbert, is generally accepted as the year of schism?

2 How many plants are referred to in the Scriptures 93, 130, 345, 790?

3 When was Lammas Day in the medieval English ecclesiastical calendar.

4 What name is given to the decorated screen which separates the sanctuary from the main body of the building in both Uniate and Orthodox Greek Churches?

5 How many Wise Men who followed the star to Bethlehem are referred to in the Gospels?

6 What is the official name of Westminster Abbey?

7 What military rank is held by the Commander of the Swiss Guards:
Major, Colonel, Brigadier, General?

8 What was the occasion of Verdi's *Requiem*?

9 What French monastic Order, founded in the eleventh century, had three houses in England – at Aldenbury, Creswell, and Grosmont?

10 Whose famous prayer is the following:
'Teach us, Good Lord, to serve Thee as Thou deservest;
To give, and not to count the cost;
To fight and not to heed the wounds;
To toil and not to seek for rest;
To labour and not to ask for reward,
Save that of knowing that we do Thy Will'?

Q98

1   On which island off the
    Northumberland coast did
    St. Aidan found his See in
    635?

2   What is the hierarchial title
    of the occupant of 22
    Binney Street, London W1?

3   What three Greek terms do
    theologians use to distin-
    guish between the *adoration*
    due to God, the *veneration*
    paid to the Blessed Virgin,
    and the *devotion* given to the
    saints?

4   In 1864 Pius IX condemned
    various trends of his time
    including pantheism, social-
    ism, civil marriage, secular
    education and indifferen-
    tism etc. What is this
    document commonly called?

5   What were the officials
    (cantor, archivist, sacrist,
    cellarer etc) of medieval
    monasteries collectively
    called?

6   Is a Church declaration of
    nullity of a marriage the
    equivalent of a divorce?

7   What were the first four
    great councils in the history
    of the Catholic Church?

8   Whose visions led to the
    discovery of the foundations
    of an isolated house on a
    high hill behind Ephesus
    (Efes in modern Turkey)

said to have been the home
of the Blessed Virgin Mary
after the death of Christ?

9   Which Bishop of
    Philadelphia, USA, was
    canonized in 1977?

10 In the nineteenth century a
    Miss Gardener married a
    man who became President
    of the United States of
    America. As a Catholic she
    was the first adherent of the
    Faith to enjoy shared occu-
    pancy of the White House.
    Who was the President?

Q99

1   What is the Papal processional chair called?

2   What name is given to the financial support, spontaneous or fixed, of the clergy?

3   Name the fifteenth century manuscript of an Englishwoman, wife 'to a worshipful burgess of Lynne', previously only been known to have existed, which was sent to the V & A Museum in London for repairs to its original binding in 1936 and identified by Emily Hope Allen, connoisseur of medieval English mysticism.

4   What is a priest who is authorised to hear confessions and grant absolution anywhere called?

5   Which French novelist, who wrote in bed, said: 'A performance of Wagner at Bayreuth is a trivial thing compared with the celebration of High Mass in Chartres Cathedral'?

6   Who said, and where: 'Tell the world not to wait. It needs to convert. When God comes He will not be joking'?

7   What did the Santo Domingo Government erect to commemorate the five hundredth anniversary of the arrival of Christopher Columbus, and what was its shape?

8   What is the official daily newspaper of the Vatican?

9   What lay community, founded by Andrea Riccardi in 1968 and, inspired by Vatican II and Pope John Paul II's Assisi summit in 1986, now numbers over 15,000 members worldwide and organises high-level inter-faith dialogue?

10 What word is missing from this sentence of Chesterton, quoting Belloc: 'Thomas More died for the - - - - - - because it was part of the Truth; not because it was his favourite part or, to him and his friends, a particularly sympathetic or popular part'?

Q100

1. What Catholic subject did Muslim Turkey picture on one of its 1917 Relief postage stamps?

2. Of whom did Professor W.R. Chambers say that: 'In English or in Latin - - - - - - - - - - - - was, during the latter half of the fourteenth century and the whole of the 15th, probably the most widely read in England of all the English writers'?

3. What is the Sabbatine Privilege?

4. What is the literal meaning of the word Pentecost?

5. What were the four main mendicant Orders of friars in the Middle Ages?

6. What single word is missing from this sentence taken from Vatican II's Pastoral Constitution on the Church in the Modern World (*Gaudium et Spes*): '- - - - - - - - - - is the most secret core and sanctuary of a man. There he is alone with God, whose voice echoes in his depths. In a wonderful manner - - - - - - - - - - reveals that law which is fulfilled by love of God and neighbour'?

7. What is the difference between an *Imprimatur* and a *Nihil Obstat* among the preliminary pages of a book?

8. What was the title of the 'Play-Cycle on the Life of Our Lord and Saviour Jesus Christ' written for radio by Dorothy L. Sayers and broadcast by the BBC between December 1941 and October 1942?

9. By what name were Roman Catholics identified in Dryden's 1681 political satire *Absalom and Achitophel*?

10. 'Oh, Lord, shall I die at all? Yes! Why then, O Lord, why not now?' Whose last words were these?

Answers

1 – PAGE 3

1 The chapel of Nicholas V.
2 Doxology.
3 Christian (In *A Pilgrim's Progress*.)
4 The Congregation of the Holy Cross.
5 Dolores Hart. (b.1938).
6 *Gargantua and Pantagruel* (Rabelais).
7 The Book of Kells (In the library of Trinity College, Dublin).
8 James II. (By, of course, Charles II.)
9 His ring (*The Ingoldsby Legends* Rev. R.H. Barnham).
10 Mr. Bloom (*Ulysses*).

2 – PAGE 4

1 On the first Sunday following the full moon on or after March 21st.
2 Benedict IX (It used to be said that he was twelve, but more recently scholars have reckoned him to have been about twenty when elected in 1032).
3 The Blessed Dominic Barberi C.P.
4 Eight (St. Matthew 5. 3–10).
5 Sophia University.
6 Fr. Richard Neuhaus.
7 Piers Paul Reid.
8 Leo XIII (In 1898).
9 The Mozarabic Liturgy.
10 St. Teresa of Avila (1515–1582) in Letter 92, To Don Rodrigo de Moya).

3 – PAGE 5

1 Victory.
2 Modernism.
3 Porter, Reader, Exorcist, Acolyte.
4 Sub-deacon, Deacon, Priest, Bishop.
5 *The Magic Flute*.
6 John Milton (1608–1674)

7 Sister Josefa Menèndes.
8 St. Jerome (342–420)
9 Roam.
10 St. John Fisher (1469–1535)

4 – PAGE 6

1 The eleventh century (1054)
2 Rwanda.
3 *Salve Regina*, (Hail Holy Queen).
4 The Cuban missile crisis which brought Russia and the United States to the brink of nuclear war.
5 *Notre Dame* (Paris).
6 Barrister.
7 1944 (Florence Li Tim-oi, by the Anglican Bishop of Hong Kong).
8 Cardinal Terence James Cooke.
9 Glossolalia.
10 Charlie Chaplin.

5 – PAGE 7

1 Leon Joseph Suenens.
2 Gregory XIII. (1502–1585)
3 Peter's Pence.
4 War (Conquest), Famine, Pestilence and Death.
5 The fourth Sunday before Christmas.
6 St. Alban.
7 The Angelus.
8 13.
9 *Ad limina*.
10 Ecstasy.

6 – PAGE 8

1 The Council of Florence.
2 Sea of Chinnereth, Lake of Gennesareth, Lake of Tiberias.
3 Cardinal. (Pope Paul III had created him Cardinal while he was in prison.)
4 St. Gerard Majella.
5 119–133. (Hebrew 120–134.) (Probably recited by pilgrims going up to Jerusalem.)
6 The Visitation.
7 The Ambrosian Rite.
8 *Raca* or *Raqa* (meaning fool, nit-wit, or empty-headed).
9 Septuagesima.
10 Bruce Marshal (From *All Glorious Within*).

7 – PAGE 10

1 The World, the Flesh and the Devil.
2 Those in Religious Orders take solemn vows; those in Religious Congregations take simple vows.
3 Abjuration.
4 Because of its *Bulla*, or leaden seal.
5 Bella Fleace. (*Bella Fleace gave a Party*, From *Work Suspended*).
6 St. Raymund de Peñafort.
7 Love.
8 Brother Lawrence. His conversations and letters were subsequently published as *The Practice of the Presence of God*.
9 Gilbert Keith Chesterton (1874–1936)
10 Meister Eckhart (1260–1327)

8 – PAGE 11

1 Hammer.
2 Counsel for the dying; in particular a written guide for the priest in his ministry to the dying.
3 The Monday and Tuesday before Ash Wednesday.
4 Teilhard de Chardin (1881–1955)
5 Algeria.
6 Scriptural Tropology.
7 Wormwood. (From C.S. Lewis's *The Screwtape Letters*).
8 Transubstantiation.
9 St. James the Greater.
10 Albigenses or Albigensians

9 – PAGE 12

1 Benedicta of the Cross.
2 Abbasiyah, Egypt.
3 'I am the Virgin of the Poor.'
4 Their badges showed two crossed palms.
5 A Eucharistic Congress.
6 The Edict of Milan.
7 Peter Abelard (1079–1142)
8 Cardinal Herbert Vaughan (1832–1903)
9 Dismas.
10 '... never send to know for whom the bell tolls; it tolls for thee.'

10 – PAGE 13

1 S. Pietro in Vincoli.
2 Caldey.
3 The Oratorians.
4 Camaldolese.
5 Richard Crawshaw. (*Upon Our Savour's Tomb, Wherein Never Man was Laid*. From *Steps to the Temple*, 1633.)
6 The 1850s. (1853. Under Pius IX.)
7 Hylozoism.
8 Honorius I. (Pope from 625–638)
9 King George V in 1910.
10 Fénelon (1651–1715), Archbishop of Cambrai.

11 – PAGE 14

1 Pope John XXIII in the inaugural address at Vatican II.
2 *The Way of a Pilgrim.*
3 1970.
4 Edmund Bonner (1500–1569).
5 At one i.e. to reconcile. (In time it came to denote the action by which such reconciliation was affected.)
6 Because He was heading for Jerusalem. (Luke 9: 52–53)
7 Cardinal Ratzinger in *The Limits of Papacy.*
8 The Agony in the Garden; The Scourging at the Pillar; The Crowning with Thorns; The Carrying of the Cross; The Crucifixion.
9 Hilaire Belloc (1870–1953).
10 George Rose in Fredrick Rolfe's *Hadrian the Seventh.*

12 – PAGE 15

1 Spy Wednesday, Maundy Thursday, Good Friday, Holy Saturday.
2 Margaret Haughery (1814–1882).
3 The little box containing the relics which is placed inside the reliquary.
4 Tutiorism or Rigorism, two words for the same concept.
5 1858 (11th February).
6 Palm Sunday.
7 The Truce (or Peace) of God.
8 Albania.
9 Tritheism.
10 Robert Hugh Benson (1871–1914).

13 – PAGE 16

1 Enrique Irazoque.

2 Pax Romana.
3 1969.
4 1973.
5 A fox. (Luke 13:32)
6 John of Plano Caprini. (The other two contemporary Eastern travellers were Dominicans.)
7 Dario Fo.
8 Boznia-Herzegovina (in Western Herzegovina).
9 A small skull cap worn by the hierarchy. (The Pope's is white, a Cardinal's red and a Bishop's purple.)
10 St. Catherine of Siena.

14 – PAGE 17

1 The land of Nod (Gen. 4:16).
2 9.
3 John Henry Newman (1801–1890)
4 St. Scholastica (480–543)
5 Diocletian (245–316)
6 A paten.
7 Orange Peel.
8 The dogma of Papal Infallibility.
9 Mary Ann Glendon.
10 Oberammergau.

15 – PAGE 18

1 1992 (Dec. 9th)
2 Formosus (reigned 891–896)
3 Fr. Matthew Fox.
4 St. Stephen Harding (d. 1134)
5 To ordain women as Anglican priests.
6 A convent of Benedictine nuns of the Perpetual Adoration.
7 Titian (1478–1576)
8 Three days of a particular devotion.
9 Accidie.
10 Francis Tregian (1548–1608)

16 – PAGE 19

1 Countess of Salisbury.
2 Baptism, Confirmation, Holy Orders.
3 1978.
4 2930:4.
5 1968.
6 *Grace Abounding to the Chief of Sinners.*
7 The Pharisees to one another. (John. 12:19)
8 Rheims.
9 St. Ambrose.
10 St. Thomas Aquinas.

17 – PAGE 20

1 Yes. (In spite of an *ex cathedra* pronouncement by Pope Honorius I, that pontiff having been declared a heretic by the Third Council of Constantinople in 680.)
2 Adamites.
3 Polydorus. (In Henri Ghéon's *The Comedian and the Grace* 1925.)
4 Because of the long, pointed hood (*Capuche*) of their habit which is similar to that worn by St. Francis.
5 In a peal bells are swung while in a Carillon they are firmly bolted to a framework and struck from rows of handlevers. (A carillon ascends chromatically through at least two octaves and contains not less than twenty-three bells. The largest could contain six octaves – seventy-two bells.)
6 In the Mass.
7 Man.
8 The Golden Rose.
9 Clare Boothe Luce (Born 1903.)
10 Menologion.

18 – PAGE 21

1 Jan Hus.
2 A turnbroach.
3 *The First Legion* (Emmet Lavery)
4 *La Papessa.* (Or The Female Pope)
5 A church, or a building consecrated for religious purposes.
6 Little Nellie of God.
7 Laying violent hands on the Pope.
8 A tax paid by parishes and benefices to their See.
9 St. Bernard of Menthon (or Montjoux) (996–1081)
10 Spirit, fire.

19 – PAGE 22

1 Pamukale (Cotton Castle)
2 The Beguines.
3 Eisegesis.
4 Grace.
5 Vespers (The Scicilian Vespers).
6 The Hieronymites (i.e. after St. Jerome).
7 Homiletics.
8 Humeral veil.
9 Ninēveh (Jonah 4:11 – Jerusalem Bible).
10 Sadhu Sundar Singh.

20 – PAGE 23

1 Octave.
2 Linus.
3 Gnostic.
4 The Sayings of the Desert Fathers (Note the mixture of Greek and Latin in the term.)
5 Speaking with wisdom; Speaking with knowledge; Faith; Healing; Miracles;

Prophecy; Discerning spirits; Tongues;
Interpreting speeches.
6 St. Jerome (342–420)
7 Demons.
8 Twenty-six
9 Abraham Lincoln.
10 Walter Raleigh, Earl of Essex. (The
   books were presented to the newly
   founded Bodleian Library at Oxford.)

21 – PAGE 24

1 'Come and see.'
2 St. Margaret Mary Alacoque
   (1647–1690)
3 Because Hugh (1135–1200) of Avalon,
   Burgundy, was a Carthusian before
   being called to the Bishopric.
4 Oblate.
5 Baltimore.
6 Longinus.
7 Jean-Baptiste-Marie Vianney
   (1786–1859)
8 In the valley of Jezrahel.
9 The Anglican Clergyman Chad Varah.
10 George Herbert (1593–1633)

22 – PAGE 25

1 Low Sunday.
2 Professor Laileb.
3 Pope John XXII (1249–1334)
4 His father had been on business in
   France at the time of his son's birth and,
   on his return, changed the boy's name
   to Francisco in memory of his visit.
5 St. Basil the Great, his brother St.
   Gregory of Nyssa and St. Gregory of
   Nazianzen.
6 Conclave.
7 Amputation.
8 The Motion Picture industry.
9 Adrian VI (1582–1623) A Dutchman
   from Utrecht – Erasmus was one of his

pupils – he was only one of two Popes
in modern times to retain his
baptismal name.
10 Cardinal Richelieu (1585–1642)

23 – PAGE 26

1 The Angelus.
2 William Langland (1333–1399)
3 Peter Hebblethwaite.
4 Knill (Sir Stuart Knill and Sir John
   Knill).
5 Genuflexion.
6 The Gathering of the Manna.
7 Simeon, In the temple of Jerusalem
   when the infant Christ was presented
   (Luke 2: 22–35).
8 *Filioque.*
9 Portuguese.
10 St. Benedict.

24 – PAGE 28

1 Rome.
2 Felix V (Amadeus VIII of Saxony, Anti-
   Papacy: 1439–1449).
3 London. (In a terraced house in Brix-
   ton.)
4 St. Ann's.
5 *Quadragesimo Anno.*
6 The weekly recitation of the whole
   psalter was abolished in favour of a
   four week cycle.
7 The Blessed Ferdinand (1402–1443),
   son of John of Gaunt's daughter
   Philippa, who married King João I of
   Portugal. Another son of their union
   was Henry the Navigator.
8 ox; ass.
9 One, a small Jesuit chapel in Godavari,
   ten miles from Katmandu. It is dedicated to Our Lady of the Immaculate
   Conception.
10 *Armide.* (1777)

25 – PAGE 29

1 Cincture.
2 1833.
3 Because he was French, was in France when elected (1305), was under great pressure from the French King, Philip the Fair, and the unfavourable political conditions in Rome dissuaded him from going there.
4 Lady Marchmain in *Brideshead Revisited*.
5 Overnight.
6 Because, it is said, he was martyred by having his intestines wound out of his body on a windlass.
7 Anthropomorphism.
8 Graham Greene (1904–1992)
9 Nudity, and the physical depiction of Jesus.
10 The Rota.

26 – PAGE 30

1 AB (The one which has no forbidden donors).
2 St. Peregrine Laziosi (A thirteenth century Servite brother.)
3 *Stabat Mater*.
4 St. Anselm.
5 He changed the title to *The Feast at the House of Levi*.
6 *The Keys of the Kingdom*.
7 Docetism.
8 St. Paul of the Cross (1694–1775).
9 He was taken from his mother's womb after her death (*non natus* = not born) and as a consequence is the patron saint of midwives. (Incidentally, In Algiers his lips were pierced with a red-hot iron and sealed with a padlock to stop him from preaching.)
10 Hal.

27 – PAGE 31

1 'I am the Immaculate Conception.'
2 One of the Trinity was crucified.
3 *Kulturkampf* (Conflict of belief).
4 He gave his name to the camelia.
5 The catacombs.
6 The Vatican.
7 4,210.
8 Marie Stopes.
9 Sizm. (O.E.D.)
10 St. Athanasius. (296–373)

28 – PAGE 32

1 The St. Bartholomew Massacre.
2 A concordat.
3 Matthew, Mark and Luke.
4 An Ambo. (Apparently an old Greek word for a mountain, the sense being taken from biblical concepts such as the Sermon on the Mount and Isaiah 40:9 – 'Get thee up on a high mountain, thou that bringest good tidings to Sion')
5 The Purification or Candlemas Day, February 2nd.
6 St. Cecilia.
7 Malcolm Muggeridge
8 *Agape*.
9 Llanthony.
10 Spike Milligan.

29 – PAGE 33

1 The sense organs: eyes, ears, nostrils, lips and hands.
2 The Banns.
3 Ember days (A corruption of *Quatur tempora*).
4 The Œcumenical Patriarch of Constantinople, Head of the Eastern

Orthodox Church (Patriarch Athenagorus.)

5 Doctor Pangloss (Voltaire *Candide*).
6 Judges (4:21).
7 *The Philokalia.*
8 Marc'Antonio de Dominio, Archbishop of Spoleto (1566–1624).
9 *Foreign Correspondent* (1940).
10 A pall.

30 – PAGE 35

1 St. Angela Merici (1474–1540).
2 12.
3 Marcionites.
4 The Carmelites.
5 Universalism.
6 Franz Liszt.
7 Ronald Firbank (1886–1926).
8 In 1059 (under Pope Nicholas II.)
9 Ten grandchildren (He was consecrated in the former underground Church of Czechoslovakia).
10 The Carthusians.

31 – PAGE 36

1 *The Seven Storey Mountain.*
2 Kindness.
3 Leo III (The Isaurian).
4 Jerome Savoranola (1452–1498).
5 The Dormition.
6 Vicar of Christ.
7 Uz (or Hus).
8 St. Jerome (Letter seventy-seven).
9 Maredsous.
10 The Septuagint.

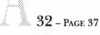

32 – PAGE 37

1 1962–65.

2 The Carmelites.
3 St. Francis Xavier (1506–1552).
4 The Diet of Worms.
5 Baruch.
6 The Huguenots.
7 Arason Jón of Holar (1484–1550). He was, apparently, an admirable Bishop in every way except that he disregarded the law of celibacy. He was executed with two of his sons.
8 John Henry Newman (Newman lost but was exonerated by the Protestant Press).
9 Indulgences.
10 St. Francis de Sales.

33 – PAGE 38

1 The Council of Constance (1415).
2 Apse.
3 The crown of thorns.
4 1960.
5 Handel's Messiah.
6 Maynooth.
7 'It is consummated' according to John; 'Father, into Thy hands I commend my spirit' according to Luke; 'Eloi, Eloi, lama sabacthani', followed by a loud cry, according to Matthew.
8 Those who pick and choose teachings according to their inclinations.
9 Henry Fonda.
10 Alexander Pope (1688–1744). From a letter to William Wycherley.

34 – PAGE 39

1 John Henry Newman (1801–1890).
2 The Premonstratensian Canons. (Or Norbertines. St. Norbert founded them at Prémontré, near Laon, France.)
3 5,480.
4 Cardinal Basil Hume.
5 A narthex.
6 December 8th.
7 Six palm (of the hand) breadths (18in or 45cm).
8 The anointed one.
9 The study of the last things (Usually Death, Judgement, Hell and Heaven, but it can be broadened to include the fate of nations and the world in general).
10 The Old Testament, or specifically II Maccabees.

35 – PAGE 40

1 St. Jane Frances de Chantal (1572–1641).
2 Quarr.
3 Sicily.
4 Papal Prefect.
5 Mother Agnes of Jesus, sister of St. Térèse.
6 nowhere ... everywhere.
7 Christ the Cornerstone.
8 Prinknash.
9 The Franciscan Friars of the Atonement.
10 Patrick O'Donovan.

36 – PAGE 42

1 Sue Ryder, Baroness Ryder of Warsaw.

2 They sport generative organs.
3 Clement VII (1478–1354)
4 They were beatified.
5 Margaret Sinclair.
6 Chris Patten.
7 Eparchy.
8 Death, Judgement, Hell and Heaven.
9 Meister Eckhart (1260–1327)
10 The Holy House of Loreto.

37 – PAGE 43

1 St. Gall. (Or Gallen.)
2 *Introibo ad altare Dei.*
3 No.
4 Dante's *Divine Comedy.*
5 *Viaticum.*
6 Bollandists.
7 Qumrān.
8 Poland (Wladyslaw Biernacki).
9 Popery.
10 James Shirley.

38 – PAGE 44

1 Maronites.
2 The Blessed José Marià Escrivà de Balaguer (1902–1975).
3 St. Francis Borgia (1510–1572).
4 Pope John XXIII of Vatican II.
5 Portugal.
6 The St. Barnabas Society.
7 Wisdom, Piety, Understanding, Counsel, Fortitude, Knowledge, Fear of the Lord.
8 The Salesians.
9 Hagiography.
10 Evil.

39 – PAGE 45

1 Arian.
2 80.
3 1984.
4 The Council of Churches for Britain and Ireland.
5 The Archbishopric of Milan.
6 The Confessions of St. Augustine.
7 The Second Spring.
8 Jean Baptiste François Pompallier (1801–1871).
9 Oblation.
10 Benediction.

40 – PAGE 46

1 Auschwitz.
2 Castel Gandolfo.
3 Graham Greene.
4 Wimbledon.
5 Prisons.
6 The late Group Captain Leonard Cheshire, VC, OM, DSO, DFC.
7 Prague's.
8 Walsingham.
9 *Papabile.*
10 Czestochowa.

41 – PAGE 47

1 A medieval manuscript or roll containing transcriptions of ecclesiastical documents.
2 Matins and Lauds on the last three days of Holy Week. They have traditionally been sung on the previous evening, with candles extinguished after each psalm, ending in darkness.
3 The exchange of spiritual for temporal things. (From Simon Magus. Acts 8: 9–24)
4 A cloister.
5 A Vicar-Apostolic.
6 The Consistory.
7 A church or cathedral which has been awarded this title by the Pope. It indicates certain formal privileges of honour.
8 A reredos, retable or altar-piece.
9 The Rephaim (Deut. 3:11).
10 Sir Arnold Lunn (1888–1974).

42 – PAGE 48

1 Your Grace.
2 The Assumption of the Blessed Virgin (1950).
3 Bishop Eamonn Casey.
4 Charity
Joy,
Peace,
Patience,
Benignity,
Goodness,
Longanimity,
Mildness,
Faith,
Modesty,
Continency and
Chastity
5 Ellis Peters.
6 Pius IX. (Thirty-two years).
7 Braga.
8 Frequent reception of Holy Communion.
9 James I.
10 Tubal (Setúbal).

43 – PAGE 49

1 Mgr. Lefebvre.
2 Saragossa.
3 Cardinal Manning (When he was an Anglican clergyman).
4 St. Thomas Aquinas. (Playing a trick on the Saint a brother Religious excitedly called him to a window to see cows flying. He hurried there but when he saw nothing he made this historic rejoinder.)
5 Buddhism.
6 *The Satin Slipper.*
7 *Apostolicae Curae.*
8 Fra Angelico.
9 *The Hound of Heaven.*
10 Galileo (for teaching that the earth revolves around the sun).

44 – PAGE 50

1 Salamanca.
2 Robert Louis Stevenson with his famous philippic, and Charles Warren Stoddard with his book *The Lepers of Molokai.*
3 Seventy-five.
4 Camels (There are two of them).
5 Sister Magdalene of Jesus.
6 He commanded the night club *The Garden of Eden* to be removed, by the power of the Holy Spirit, from its site in an Edinburgh street to Bass Rock in the Firth of Forth – and it was. (In Bruce Marshall's novel *Father Malachy's Miracle.*)
7 The Uniate churches.
8 Dorian Gray.
9 Goree.
10 a) St. Peter's Basilica, Rome. b) St. Paul's Cathedral, London. c) The Cathedral of Seville, Spain.

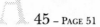

45 – PAGE 51

1 Frankinscense.
2 1099.
3 Prudence, Justice, Fortitude, Temperance.
4 The Merciful Knight. (One of his relations had been murdered and, considering it his duty to avenge the crime, he went after the slayer and met him in an alleyway. The man threw himself on the ground with his arms outstretched in the form of a cross and begged mercy in the name of Christ whereupon John Gualbert spared him).
5 The Inquisition.
6 He deplored it. (Indeed he issued a Bull revoking it and excommunicated the barons).
7 George Eliot (1819–1880).
8 St. Thomas More (1478–1535) (In *Utopia*).
9 The second decade (1817) by Benedict Marcellin Champagnat (1789–1840).
10 St. Clement of Alexandria.

46 – PAGE 52

1 St. Thomas Aquinas (1225–1274).
2 1979.
3 No. It may only be administered when one is in danger of death from natural causes.
4 The White Fathers.
5 The Church Militant; The Church Suffering; The Church Triumphant.
6 Bishop of Rome,
Vicar of Christ,
Successor of the Prince of the Apostles,
Supreme Pontiff of the Universal Church,
Patriarch of the West,

Primate of Italy,
Archbishop and Metropolitan of the
    Roman Province,
Sovereign of the State of Vatican City
    and
Servant of the Servants of God.
7 He was banished to Lyons in France by
   the Emperor Caligula.
8 Mixt (or mixtum).
9 Gerard Manley Hopkins (1844–1889).
10 An elephant (which was included in
   one day's sight-seeing with the relics of
   St. Barbara).

4 Canon Law.
5 Clerks Regular.
6 Hunchback.
7 Animism.
8 Palatine, Capitoline, Aventine,
   Caelian, Esquiline, Viminal and
   Quirinal.
9 *Pacem in Terris.*
10 St. Thomas Aquinas. (From the *Vita
   Sancto Thomae Aquinatus* by Peter
   Calo.)

47 – PAGE 53

1 That they shall be counted the Children of God.
2 By Baptism.
3 Celibacy.
4 From different styles of turf (peat)
   cutting in Ulster. Catholics used
   spades with the lug on the left side,
   Protestants with the lug on the right.
5 Theophany (From the Greek *Theopha-
   nia* meaning an appearance by God.
6 The Society of the Holy Child Jesus.
7 Outside, presumably. The Jews at the
   time did not permit burial inside the
   city except in the case of their kings,
   and they had refused to acknowledge
   Christ's Kingship.
8 *Sacrobosco.*
9 St. Ethelreda's Ely Place, Holborn.
10 *The Cloud of Unknowing.*

49 – PAGE 56

1 21.
2 Ampullae.
3 Catherine de Medici (1519–1589).
4 Martin.
5 Mehmet Ali Agca (who had attempted
   to assassinate His Holiness in May
   1981).
6 Jozef Mindszenty (1892–1975).
7 *That Was The Week That Was.*
8 On the door of the castle church at
   Wittenburg. (It was the 16th of Martin
   Luther's ninty-five theses.)
9 Mariazell.
10 Gilbert Keith Chesterton.

48 – PAGE 54

1 Nicholas Wiseman (1802–1865).
2 St. Germanus (496–576). (*Saint-
   Germain-des-Pres* and a purée of fresh
   pea soup with whole fresh peas and
   chervil added.)
3 *The Shepherd* by Hermas.

A 50 – PAGE 57

1 *Autocephali.*
2 Cheyne Walk (No. 104).
3 Thirty-three.
4 His talents as a linguist (He is said to have been able to speak and write thirty-eight languages perfectly, thirty more or less perfectly, and fifty dialects of these).
5 The Cenacle (Or *Coenaculum*).
6 St. Lawrence of Brindisi (1559–1619).
7 John McCloskey (1810–1885) (fourth Bishop and second Archbishop of New York).
8 Louis Grignion de Montfort (1673–1747).
9 Myrrh.
10 Sir Arthur Quiller-Couch (1863–1944) (*On Reading the Bible II*, Cambridge Lecture April 24th 1918).

A 51 – PAGE 59

1 Walter Pidgeon.
2 A Diatessaron.
3 St. Francis of Assisi.
4 *Ipso facto* excommunication.
5 The calumnator can only receive absolution from the Pope himself (except at the point of death).
6 Lloyd C. Douglas.
7 93.
8 In the Cyclades Islands, Greek Archipelago.
9 (Alfred) Joyce Kilmer (1886–1918).
10 Henry Vaughan (1622–1695).

A 52 – PAGE 60

1 *A Sleep of Prisoners* (Christopher Fry).

2 She who points the way.
3 The Dyptychs.
4 1621. Governor Bradford of the Plymouth colony appointed a day for public praise after harvest. In 1789 Washington made the last Thursday in November the Day of National Observance.
5 St. Mary of the Angels.
6 Dr. (afterwards Cardinal) Vaughan (1832–1903).
7 The man must have completed his sixteenth year, and the woman her fourteenth.
8 An albino.
9 Bell, book and candle.
10 St. John Chrysostom (347–407).

A 53 – PAGE 62

1 *The Labyrinthine Ways.*
2 Herman Melville (1819–1891).
3 A dominicale.
4 St. Christopher.
5 The Melchite Rite.
6 Pope Pius X died.
7 The fourth Sunday after Easter (Because the Introit begins *Cantate Domino*).
8 Antonio Canov (1757–1822).
9 To eliminate all reference to the Jews.
10 'Gothic' and 'Goths'.

A 54 – PAGE 63

1 Ben Jonson (1573–1637).
2 Papistry.
3 In a Potting Shed (From his 1957 play *The Potting Shed*).
4 Spanish.
5 November 30th.
6 St. Joan of Arc (The canonization followed under Benedict XV on 9th May 1920).
7 Enrico Caruso. (1873–1921).

8 Anyone related by blood to the first or second degree to any living cardinal.
9 Eugene III (Bernardo Pignatelli, elected 1145 and died 1153).
10 Joseph Conrad (1857–1924). (All quotes are from his letters).

controversial English Franciscan).
5 Cardinal Manning (1807–1892).
6 Gog and Magog.
7 Thomas a Kempis (1380–1471).
8 Guadalupe.
9 Heortology.
10 The 'poop', or 'after', deck ('Poop' from puppets, or life-like figures).

55 – PAGE 65

1 A *baldacchino* or *ciborium*.
2 God will do nothing without man. If God works a miracle, he does it through man.
3 Bogota, Colombia.
4 Francis Bacon (1909–1992).
5 Metempsychosis.
6 St. Dunstan (909–988).
7 The Blue Laws (Because the front of the format they appeared in was blue). As an example, one provided that no husband should kiss his wife, and no wife her husband, on a Sunday: 'The party at fault being punished at the discretion of the magistrates').
8 Father Bartolomé de las Cusas (1474–1566). (His father had accompanied Columbus on his second voyage and brought back an Indian boy as a servant for his son. This started his life-long devotion to the cause of the Indians.)
9 A communal Sunday walk during which the monks converse.
10 *The State of Innocence and the Fall of Man* (A drama).

57 – PAGE 67

1 403,173.
2 Sacred Scripture.
3 His jewelled tiara.
4 Pius XI. (Within two years Italian Catholics were being told by the Vatican to disassociate themselves from Fascism).
5 Nuns are under solemn vows (generally enclosed) while sisters have taken simple vows.
6 Pizzaro had treacherously executed the Incan King Atahuallpa after extracting a roomful of gold out of his people for his release. (July/August 1533.)
7 A heresy hunter.
8 'Save' or 'Never leave'.
9 Richard Langhorne (1635–1679).
10 They are all medieval heresies.

58 – PAGE 68

1 A dalmatic.
2 The Devil's Advocate.
3 The Abbey of Bec.
4 The Order of Merit.
5 St. Bernard of Clairvaux (1090–1153).
6 Paralipomenon.
7 The *Labarum*.
8 William Russell Grace (1832–1904) of *Grace Lines Shipping Company* (Mayor of New York 1880–1888).
9 Polemics.
10 St. Aelred of Rievaulx (1109–1167).

56 – PAGE 66

1 No.
2 *Sister Beatrice* (1901).
3 To address the United Nations in New York.
4 Ockam's Razor (After William Ockham, or Occam (1285–1349) a

59 – PAGE 69

1 St. Raphael, St Michael and St. Gabriel.
2 Ronald Knox (1888–1957).
3 The Vatican Bank.
4 Thurification.
5 Frederick William Faber (1814–1863).
6 Trevor Howard.
7 Four and a half years (four years, seven months and nine days.)
8 Pellegra.
9 Cecil B. de Mille (1881–1959).
10 St. Teresa of Avila (1515–1582).

60 – PAGE 70

1 Croagh Patrick.
2 Rere-dorters. (They were usually lighted, partitioned and provided with clean hay.)
3 Antiphonal.
4 *Corpus Christi* (Instituted in 1264).
5 1972 (September 14th)
6 Edmund Ignatius Rice (1762–1844).
7 *Académie Française.*
8 The Maronite Rite.
9 Henry Stuart (1725–1807), Younger brother of Charles Edward Stuart (Bonnie Prince Charlie) and grandson of King James II and VII. He became the Cardinal Bishop of Frascati in 1761. George III gave him an annuity when his lands were taken by the French and in gratitude he left the crown jewels of James II to George IV. His papers were bought by George IV and are now in the British Museum. He was the last of the male line.)
10 Exogamy.

61 – PAGE 71

1 Dietrich Bonhoeffer (1906–1945).
2 Gadarenes.
3 They were elected by acclamation before balloting.
4 A chasuble.
5 A monstrance or *ostensorium.*
6 Queen Christina Alexandra (1626–1689).
7 A sycamore (Lk. 19:4).
8 Evelyn Waugh (1902–1966).
9 Vespers.
10 Purgatory.

62 – PAGE 72

1 C.S. Lewis (1898–1963).
2 Queen Margaret (1045–1093).
3 Fall.
4 In the mouth of the first fish that he should catch in the lake (Mt. 17:27).
5 Armand-Jean le Bouthillier de Rancé (1626–1700).
6 *Acta Sancta Sedis.*
7 He was not a priest (Indeed, he was the last such person to receive the red hat.)
8 The Cisalpine Club.
9 *Santa Croce in Gerusalemme.*
10 Sarabaites and Gyrovagues.

63 – PAGE 73

1 Because it was generally believed until well into the Middle Ages that at Pentecost each of the Apostles had contributed one of the twelve articles.
2 *La Grande Chartreuse* (fourteen miles north of Grenoble).
3 The Sisters of Charity of St. Vincent de Paul.

4   Thomas Merton (1915–1968).
5   *Veni Creator Spiritus.*
6   At Subiaco (twenty-five miles from Tivoli.)
7   Subreption is the supression of facts; Obreption is a positive allegation of what is false.
8   The dioceses nearest Rome viz. Albano, Frascati, Palestrina, Rufina, Ostia, Porto and Santa Ostia, (united in 1120) Sabina and Poggio Mireto (divided in 1841, reunited in 1925), and Velletri.
9   An alb is an ankle-length, narrow-sleeved, girded tunic.
    A surplice is a half-length, wide-sleeved, ungirded, laced tunic.
    A rochet is a half-length, narrow-sleeved, ungirded tunic. All are white and were traditionally made of linen.
10 In the church of *Santa Croce*, Florence.

64 – PAGE 74

1   Portuguese.
2   François du Tremblay or Père Joseph – *L'Éminence Grise* to Richelieu's *Éminence Rouge.*
3   The ordination of women to the Church of England priesthood.
4   Advent.
5   A large fan used to keep insects away from the Sacred Species, and the priest, mostly during a procession.
6   The *Passiflora*, or Passion Flower.
    The five stamens are the five wounds.
    The three stigmas, the three nails.
    The style of the pistil, the flogging column.
    The corona, the crown of thorns or halo of glory.
    The digitate, or fingered leaves, the hands of the multitude.
    The coiled tendrils, the flogging cords.
    The five sepals and five petals, the ten disciples – Peter and Judas being omitted.

7   Louis IX (1214–1270).
8   The Amice.
9   G.K. Chesterton in The Defendant.
10 St. Ephraim (306–373).

65 – PAGE 76

1   Angelus Silesius (1624–1677).
2   Americanism.
3   The Eastern Churches use leavened bread.
4   St. Albertus Magnus or St. Albert the Great (1206–1280).
5   To admonish the sinner,
    To instruct the ignorant,
    To counsel the doubtful,
    To comfort the sorrowful,
    To bear wrongs patiently,
    To forgive all injuries and
    To pray for the living and the dead.
6   St. John the Baptist (Jn, 1:29).
7   Carfin.
8   Crozier and ring.
9   Church.
10 The Secretary of State.

66 – PAGE 77

1   The sixteenth century.
2   Munich (München).
3   The Blue Army.
4   The Pallium.
5   Pagan (from the Latin for a 'country-man') implies a lack of interest in religion, whereas heathen suggests hostility.
6   Cardinal Nicholas Wiseman (1802–1865).
7   Matins, Lauds, Prime, Terce, Sext, None, Vespers and Compline.
8   'Theirs is the kingdom of heaven.' (Mt. 5:3 & 5:10).
9   Avignon.
10 Soubirous.

67 – PAGE 78

1 Elizabeth Seaton (1774–1821) (Canonized 1975).
2 Ciborium.
3 James Tissot.
4 In 1623 for crime, though it lingered on for civil offences until 1723.
5 Spires.
6 Torquato Tasso.
7 The *Te Deum*.
8 Francis Thompson (1859–1907) (*In No Strange Land*).
9 The Biretta.
10 The Society of St. Vincent de Paul.

68 – PAGE 79

1 The *Asperges* or in Eastertide the *Vide Aquam*.
2 Celia Copplestone (In T.S. Eliot's *The Cocktail Party*).
3 1980 (17th October).
4 *Tannhäuser*.
5 Terror.
6 No (A distinction or office is bestowed and the title goes with it).
7 Ain Karim.
8 The Congregation for the Doctrine of the Faith.
9 Stylites.
10 Robert Burton (1577–1640) in *The Anatomy of Melancholy*, writing as Democritus Junior.

69 – PAGE 80

1 Pius VI.
2 The original name of the Franciscans. The name commemorates St. Francis's vision on Mount Alverna in which he saw a seraph impressing the stigmata on his body.
3 Mussolini. (Born in the north of Italy; Mussolini means 'muslin maker'; vengeance those who frustrated his ambition of *Mare Nostrum*; Hitler his inspiration.)
4 Brendan Behan.
5 St. Veronica wipes the face of Jesus.
6 2,600.
7 St. Cyril & St. Methodius (ninth century).
8 The Holy Trinity.
9 St. Roch, or Rock (fourteenth century).
10 Margery Kempe (fifteenth century).

70 – PAGE 81

1 John Henry Newman (1801–1890) (In *Apologia Pro Vita Sua*).
2 The Way.
3 Knock.
4 Antioch.
5 George Herbert (1593–1633).
6 Shibboleth (OED definition = a test word, principle, behaviour or opinion).
7 King Frederick II of Prussia (Protestant) and The Empress Catherine II of Russia (Orthodox).
8 Pius IX and Leo XIII.
9 To signify that the blessing is Christ's and not the priest's own.
10 Teresa Neuman (born Good Friday 1898 – died 1962).

71 – PAGE 83

1 St. Januarius (or Gennarus) of whom we know nothing, except through the Venerable Bede who suggests that he died circa 305 during the Diocletian persecutions.

2 Latin, *Pons* = a bridge. *Pontifex* = a bridge maker.
3 After.
4 David Alton.
5 St. Oliver Plunket, Archbishop of Armagh.
6 Castel Gandolfo (Which is also the Papal summer palace). It is eighteen miles south-east of Rome.
7 Pascal (1623–1662) (*Pensee* 7).
8 The Acts of the Apostles, 12.13. (The servant of Mary, the mother of John Mark, who answered Peter's knock when the angel had released him from prison).
9 A Coadjutor Bishop.
10 St. Peter Claver.

72 – PAGE 84

1 St. Malachy (1094–1148)
2 Petrus Romanus.
3 The cock.
4 The Alexandrine rite.
5 Roy Campbell (1901–1957) (He was killed in a motor accident near Setùbal, Portugal, while returning from an Easter Mass).
6 Catechumen.
7 Christ.
8 I never give God thanks for loving me, because he cannot help it; whether He would or no it is His nature to.
9 a) Ghibellines. b) Guelphs.
10 Giuseppe Mazzini (1805–1872).

73 – PAGE 86

1 'Your Holiness' or 'Most Holy Father'.
2 Celestine V (In 1294). He was a hermit who wanted to return to his hermitage.
3 Decalogue.
4 Valladolid.

5 The Basilica of St. John Lateran.
6 Jaime Sin.
7 George Spenser, or Father Ignatius of St. Paul, C.P. (1799–1849).
8 Taizé.
9 Virgins.
10 QUEST.

74 – PAGE 87

1 *Theotokos* (God-bearer).
2 1927.
3 Westminster's African, Asian and Caribbean Committee.
4 Spikenard.
5 Oil from the lamp at the Holy Sepulchre.
6 A Primate.
7 Quietism.
8 The Paraguay Reductions.
9 Shakespeare.
10 St. Bonaventure (1221–1274).

75 – PAGE 88

1 Gerard Manley Hopkins (1844–1889).
2 A Pyx.
3 Aramaic.
4 Dom Bede Griffiths.
5 An imposed discipline.
6 'Your Eminence'.
7 The Immaculate Conception of Our Lady.
8 St. Genevieve (420–500).
9 Jansenism.
10 Kedron.

76 – PAGE 89

1 Pius IX.
2 The Act of Six Articles.
3 The *Magnificat.*
4 A colporteur.
5 Creed.
6 Fossors (Or Fossarians) They appear to have been considered minor clergy.
7 The Muratorian Canon (Westcott text, 1889). The surviving document, which is said to be a bad eighth century translation of the original Greek, is held in the Biblioteca Ambrosiana in Milan.
8 The Sweetheart Abbey (1275): It was also called the New Abbey Pow and was about eight miles from Dumfries.
9 Gugliemo Marconi (1874–1937), the inventor of radio.
10 The Curé d'Ars (1786–1859).

77 – PAGE 90

1 Chair.
2 In northern Italy (Trento in the Trentino).
3 Mrs. Stuart Moore.
4 St. Zachary and St. Elizabeth.
5 The Carmelites.
6 George Williams (1821–1905).
7 Because he wanted them to have the spirit of St. Francis de Sales.
8 St. John Ogilvie (1580–1615).
9 John Paul I.
10 Because the Greek word for fish, *icthus,* is composed of the opening letters of the words *Iesus Christos Theou Huios Soter* – Jesus Christ, God's Son, Saviour.

78 – PAGE 91

1 John Wyclif (1324–1384).
2 Because they have been ordained according to the Edwardian Ordinal (Edward VI) which changed the traditional and accepted ritual and was ruled by Leo XIII to be so deficient as to make Anglican orders null and void.
3 Recusant (From Latin = to refuse, be unwilling).
4 255.
5 Five (Hertfordshire, North London, East London, West London and Central London).
6 A holiday, religiously observed, happening every week.
7 Melchizedeck.
8 Matthew Talbot (1856–1925).
9 Matteo Ricci (1552–1610).
10 Sacrament.

79 – PAGE 92

1 Stole.
2 Acosmism.
3 Father Brown.
4 Dutch.
5 Gregorian Chant or Plainchant.
6 From Latin *capella* = a cape. When St. Martin divided his military cloak – *cappa* – and gave half to the beggar at the gate of Amiens, he wrapped the other half round his shoulders thus making a cape – *capella.* This cape, or its representation, afterwards accompanied the Frankish kings in their wars and the tent which sheltered it also became known as the *capella.* In this tent Mass was celebrated by the military chaplains – *capellani.*
Subsequently any oratory where Mass was celebrated was called *capella* or, in French, *chapelle.*
7 Julian of Norwich (1342–1413).
8 Exegesis.
9 Lutheran.
10 Rebellion.

80 – PAGE 93

1 *Augustinus.*
2 Primate of Ireland.
3 Amos (Subject of the first of the Old Testament prophetic books).
4 George Townsend D.D.
5 The Apostleship of the Sea.
6 Supremacy of State over Church.
7 Golgotha (Lk. 23.33).
8 Apostolic.
9 Gaius (or Caius) (Reigned 83–96) and Soter (Reigned 167–175).
10 Richard Watson Dixon (1833–1900).

81 – PAGE 94

1 Despair,
Presumption,
Impenitence (or a fixed determination not to repent),
Obstinacy,
Resisting the known truth and
Envy of another's spiritual welfare.
2 Mount Mellary.
3 Antonio Gaudi (1852–1926).
4 St Francis of Assisi's.
5 Members of the Religious Order of Friars founded by St. Francis of Padua.
6 50 (Hebrew 51).
7 8th September.
8 Ephesus,
Smyrna,
Pergamum,
Thyatira,
Sardis,
Philadelphia and
Laodicea.
9 St. Louis, the French Embassy Church.
10 Stupidity.

82 – PAGE 95

1 The Pentateuch.
2 St. Bruno (1033–1101).
3 In Cologne, Germany.
4 Julian of Norwich (1342–1413).
5 St. Rose of Lima she was canonized in 1671 (1586–1617).
6 Pride, Avarice, Lust, Anger, Gluttony, Envy and Sloth.
7 Nicholas Breakspear, Adrian IV (1100–1159).
8 Because in Genesis 3:7 it reads that Adam and Eve 'made themselves breeches' instead of donning fig-leaves.
9 Our Lady of Gethsemani, Kentucky.
10 John Milton (1608–1674).

83 – PAGE 96

1 Meekness.
2 A Cope.
3 Lough Derg (Also known as St. Patrick's Purgatory).
4 St. Bernadine of Sienna (1380–1444). He made much use of the symbol IHS.
5 St. Jan Sarkander (1576–1620).
6 The Canon.
7 Lord Macaulay (1800–1859).
8 Titus Oates (1649–1705).
9 Eighteen (Lk. 13:4).
10 An Oratario.

84 – Page 98

1 Angels,
   Archangels,
   Virtues,
   Powers,
   Principalities,
   Dominations,
   Thrones,
   Cherubim and
   Seraphim.
2 The Order of the Visitation.
3 John II (reigned 533–535).
4 To give food to the Hungry,
   To give drink to the thirsty.
   To clothe the naked.
   To shelter the homeless,
   To visit the sick,
   To visit those in prison and
   To bury the dead.
5 The Lateran Treaty.
6 *Aggiornamento.*
7 Day of Judgement.
8 Brindle St. Joseph, Near Houghton, Lancashire in 1786.
9 Pontifical Universities.
10 Walter Hilton (d. 1396).

85 – Page 99

1 *Jesus Charitas* (The Little Brothers of Jesus).
2 Leonardo da Vinci's *Last Supper.*
3 St. Matthias.
4 St. Frances Cabrini (1850–1917). She was Italian born, but a naturalised U.S. citizen. She was canonized in 1946.
5 1997.
6 The *Gloria in Excelsis.*
7 Adoptionism.
8 A Thurible or censer.
9 Amen.
10 *The Imitation of Christ* by Thomas à Kempis, from the translation by Ronald Knox.

86 – Page 100

1 A reproduction of St. Veronica's veil.
2 Anathema.
3 At the Council of Elvira (Spain) 295–302.
4 Victoria Gillick.
5 1972.
6 Chicago.
7 The Huguenots.
8 Four: at the Incarnation; at the Visitation; on discovering Jesus in the temple and at the marriage feast at Cana.
9 The Koran 4:156. (Dawood Trans.)
10 Lawrence (d. 619).

87 – Page 101

1 The Little Pebble.
2 Ecumenical.
3 The late George MacLeod. Baron MacLeod of Fuinary. He founded the Community in 1938.
4 Portugal.
5 Oscar Romero (In San Salvador).
6 Trophimus (2 Tim. 4:21).
7 The Princess of Wales.
8 Ayatollah Khomeni, Of Salman Rushdie, to Every Muslim.
9 Thirteen or Fourteen.
   one to the Romans;
   two to the Corinthians;
   one to the Galatians;
   one to the Ephesians;
   one to the Philippians;
   one to the Colossians;
   two to the Thessalonians;
   two to Timothy;
   one to Titus;
   one to Philemon and perhaps
   one to the Hebrews: The Pontifical Biblical Commission stated (1914) that St. Paul may not have been the author of the Epistle but perhaps

either a source or editor of it.
10 The Magi (*The Journey of the Magi* from
       Ariel Poems).

88 – Page 102

1 *Arabici* (or *Thanatopsychitae*).
2 'The lake that burns with fire and
     brimstone' i.e. eternal damnation.
3 Mother Teresa of Calcutta.
4 1966.
5 The Gilbertines founded by St. Gilbert
     of Sempringham (c.1083–1189).
6 St. Boniface (675–755).
7 Malcolm.
8 The Secretary calls his name three
     times and, if not answered, taps the
     deceased's head with a silver hammer.
9 Tonsure.
10 Days of prayer for harvest, protection
     and penance.
     Major = 25th April.
     Minor = Three days before the Feast of
        the Ascension.

89 – Page 103

1 He depicted Christ without a beard.
2 The Arians.
3 66.
4 St. Aldhelm (640–709).
5 The Valley of Josaphat (or
     Jehosophat) – because of Joel 3:2.
6 The saying of two masses on the one
     day.
7 Linda Darnell (1921–1965).
8 Thomas a Kempis (1380–1471).
9 St. Cunegunda (d.1035) She was
     canonized in 1200. St Henry
     (972–1023) was canonized 1152.
10 Desiderius Erasmus (1466–1536).

90 – Page 104

1 Johann Chrysostomus.
2 St. Augustine (354–430).
3 Apocryphal or the Apocrypha.
4 Tiberius Caesar (14BC–37AD).
5 Apologetics (used with a singular
     verb).
6 Apostle spoons (traditionally a spon-
     sor's baptismal gift).
7 Albino Luciani.
8 Teilhard de Chardin (*The Prayer of the
     Universe*).
9 Hans Küng.
10 King Philip II of Spain.

91 – Page 105

1 Movement for the Ordination of
     Married Men.
2 St. Pancras.
3 The first two letters of the name *Jesus*
     in Greek, (IH – iota, eta) and the first
     letter of *Christ*, (X – chi) (Thus also
     'Xmas' for 'Christmas').
4 Augustinian.
5 Milan.
6 Sir Charles Hubert Parry (1848–1918).
7 Yes (There are at least six).
8 Darkness, Nothing, Void.
9 The Pope's theologian, traditionally
     held by a Dominican.
10 St. Peter (Simon Peter or *Cephas*).

92 – PAGE 106

1 1983.
2 St. John the Evangelist, in his letters.
3 1571.
4 The Conventicle Act.
5 Cardiff.
6 The 1950s (May 20th 1955).
7 Padre Pio (1887–1968).
8 Gluttony.
9 Cosmogony.
10 Surviving account from the Chester Mystery plays, kept from 1300 to 1600.

93 – PAGE 107

1 Leonardo Boff.
2 Novena.
3 Anglican-Roman Catholic International Commission.
4 James II. (1633–1701). He fled to France in December 1688 and rallied support in Ireland. He was finally defeated at the Battle of the Boyne in 1690 and left Ireland to exile in France.
5 Brother Juniper in *The Little Flowers of St. Francis of Assisi*.
6 Primate of the Gauls.
7 The Annunciation;
   The Visitation;
   The Nativity;
   The Presentation; and
   The Finding of the Child Jesus in the Temple.
8 The fourth Sunday in Lent.
9 Death.
10 Frederick Lucas (1812–1855), M.P. for County Meath at Westminster.

94 – PAGE 108

1 Ultramontanism argues that the decisions of the Pope are absolute in themselves and not by virtue of the consent of the Church. Gallicanism claims that a Papal definition could not be valid unless subsequently, or concommitantly, it received Episcopal consent.
2 Yes.
3 Roberto Calvi.
4 St. Thomas More.
5 The discalced go barefoot, or in open sandals. The calced are shod.
6 St. Maria Goretti (1890–1902).
7 The Holy Innocents December 28th.
8 Q: Who made you? A: God made me and lives in me.
9 The Holy Grail.
10 Pius XI.

95 – PAGE 109

1 The lacerations of the Scourging cover the body.
2 A movement in the U.S. in the 1850s to proscribe Roman Catholicism. (Members, who resorted to many acts of violence, would answer, 'I don't know!' to any inquiries, even when the blood was visible on their hands.)
3 St. Joachim and St. Anne.
4 Iconium.
5 The Society for the Promotion of Christian Knowledge.
6 Pope (Saint) Hormisdas (Reigned 514–523) was the father of Pope Silverius (Reigned 536–537).
7 Potatoes.
8 Monks of the Armenian Catholic Uniate Church following the Benedictine Rule. (The Order was formed by Abbot Mechitar in 1712 and their Mother House is in Venice.)

9 Armagh. The Archbishop of Armagh is Primate of All Ireland, the Archbishop of Dublin, Primate of Ireland.
10 Hypostatic Union.

96 – PAGE 110

1 Our Lady of Guadalupe.
2 Eastern monks of the fifth century (The Sleepless Monks) who established the *laus perennis* of which our modern Perpetual Adoration is a continuation.
3 The Holy Shroud of Turin.
4 The Three Wise Men or Magi. (Balthasar, Melchior and Caspar).
5 Adolphe Tanquerey.
6 St. Servace (Servatius) (died 384).
7 Lisbon. The Estrala Basilica, built in 1780 by Queen Maria in thanksgiving for a son and heir.
8 Canisius, St. Peter Canisius, the Watchdog of the Church (1521–1597).
9 Alice Meynell (1847–1922).
10 Youth.

97 – PAGE 111

1 1054 AD.
2 130.
3 1 August, The Feast of St. Peter's Chains.
4 An Iconostasis.
5 The Gospel (St. Matthew's only) doesn't specify.
6 The Collegiate Church of St. Peter in Westminster.
7 Colonel.
8 It began as a project to the memory of Rossini but was completed and used for the Anniversary of Manzoni's death.
9 Grandmontine.
10 St. Ignatius Loyola (1491–1556).

98 – PAGE 112

1 Lindisfarne.
2 The Apostolic Exarch (Bishop) for Ukranians in Great Britain.
3 *Latria, Hyperdulia* and *Dulia.*
4 The Syllabus of Errors. (A list of eighty errors attached to the encyclical *Quanta Cura*).
5 Obedientiaries.
6 No. Nullity asserts that, owing to certain circumstances, no proper marriage was ever entered into.
7 Nicaea (325), Constantinople (381), Ephesus (431) and Chalcedon (451).
8 Anne Catherine Emmerich. (1774–1824)
9 St. John Nepomucene Neumann. (1811–1860)
10 John Tyler (1790–1862).

99 – PAGE 113

1 *Sedia Gestatoria.*
2 Stipend.
3 The Book of Margery Kempe.
4 A licentiate.
5 Marcel Proust (1871–1922).
6 The Blessed Virgin, at Medjugorje.
7 A lighthouse, in the form of a cross.
8 *L'Osservatore Romano.*
9 The Sant' Egidio Community.
10 Papacy.

100 – PAGE 114

1 A Sister of Mercy.
2 Richard Rolle.
3 A belief that the Blessed Virgin will secure the release from purgatory of souls who have been especially devoted to her.
4 Fifty days – i.e. fifty days after the Passover (In Christian usage the seventh Sunday after Easter).
5 Franciscans,
  Dominicans,
  Augustinians and
  Carmelites.
6 Conscience.
7 *Imprimatur* signifies a Bishop's approbation of a work; *Nihil Obstat* means that there is no theological reason why it should not be published.
8 *The Man Born to be King.*
9 Jebusites.
10 St. Augustine (354–430)